Cryptology

Other titles in the Crime Scene Investigations series:

Ballistics

Blackmail and Bribery

Body Farms

The Case of the Green River Killer

The Case of the Zodiac Killer

Cold Cases

The Columbine School Shootings

Computer Hacking

The Crime Scene Photographer

Criminal Profiling

Cybercrime

DNA Evidence

Fingerprinting

Forensic Art

Forensic Biology

The Forensic Entomologist

The Homicide Detective

Identity Theft

Investigating the Mafia

The John F. Kennedy Assassination

Kidnapping

K9 Police Units

The Murder of Emmett Till

The 9/11 Investigation

The O.J. Simpson Murder Trial

The Oklahoma City Bombing

Poisoning

Surveillance

Tracking Serial Killers

The Unabomber

Underwater Forensics

Cryptology

by Jenny MacKay

LUCENT BOOKS
A part of Gale, Cengage Learning

GALE
CENGAGE Learning

Detroit • New York • San Francisco • New Haven, Conn • Waterville, Maine • London

LIBRARY OF CONGRESS CATALOGING-IN-PUBLICATION DATA

MacKay, Jenny, 1978-
  Cryptology / by Jenny MacKay.
    p. cm. -- (Crime scene investigations)
  Includes bibliographical references and index.
  ISBN 978-1-4205-0140-7 (hardcover)
  1. Forensic sciences. 2. Cryptography. 3. Criminal investigation. I. Title.
  HV8073.M2193 2010
  363.25'65--dc22
                                                                2010016860

Lucent Books
27500 Drake Rd
Farmington Hills MI 48331

ISBN-13: 978-1-4205-0140-7
ISBN-10: 1-4205-0140-2

Printed in the United States of America
1 2 3 4 5 6 7 14 13 12 11 10

Printed by Bang Printing, Brainerd, MN, 1ˢᵗ Ptg., 09/2010

Contents

Foreword   6

Introduction   8
The Science of Making and Breaking Codes

Chapter 1   11
What Is Cryptology?

Chapter 2   28
How Criminals Use Cryptology

Chapter 3   45
Cracking Criminal Codes

Chapter 4   61
Hiding Data from Criminals

Chapter 5   77
The Future of Cryptology

Notes   91

Glossary   96

For More Information   98

Index   100

Picture Credits   104

About the Author   104

Foreword

The popularity of crime scene and investigative crime shows on television has come as a surprise to many who work in the field. The main surprise is the concept that crime scene analysts are the true crime solvers, when in truth, it takes dozens of people, doing many different jobs, to solve a crime. Often, the crime scene analyst's contribution is a small one. One Minnesota forensic scientist says that the public "has gotten the wrong idea. Because I work in a lab similar to the ones on *CSI*, people seem to think I'm solving crimes left and right—just me and my microscope. They don't believe me when I tell them that it's just the investigators that are solving crimes, not me."

Crime scene analysts do have an important role to play, however. Science has rapidly added a whole new dimension to gathering and assessing evidence. Modern crime labs can match a hair of a murder suspect to one found on a murder victim, for example, or recover a latent fingerprint from a threatening letter, or use a powerful microscope to match tool marks made during the wiring of an explosive device to a tool in a suspect's possession.

Probably the most exciting of the forensic scientist's tools is DNA analysis. DNA can be found in just one drop of blood, a dribble of saliva on a toothbrush, or even the residue from a fingerprint. Some DNA analysis techniques enable scientists to tell with certainty, for example, whether a drop of blood on a suspect's shirt is that of a murder victim.

While these exciting techniques are now an essential part of many investigations, they cannot solve crimes alone. "DNA doesn't come with a name and address on it," says the Minnesota forensic scientist. "It's great if you have someone in custody to match the sample to, but otherwise, it doesn't help.

That's the investigator's job. We can have all the great DNA evidence in the world, and without a suspect, it will just sit on a shelf. We've all seen cases with very little forensic evidence get solved by the resourcefulness of a detective."

While forensic specialists get the most media attention today, the work of detectives still forms the core of most criminal investigations. Their job, in many ways, has changed little over the years. Most cases are still solved through the persistence and determination of a criminal detective whose work may be anything but glamorous. Many cases require routine, even mind-numbing tasks. After the July 2005 bombings in London, for example, police officers sat in front of video players watching thousands of hours of closed-circuit television tape from security cameras throughout the city, and as a result were able to get the first images of the bombers.

The Lucent Books Crime Scene Investigations series explores the variety of ways crimes are solved. Titles cover particular crimes such as murder, specific cases such as the killing of three civil rights workers in Mississippi, or the role specialists such as medical examiners play in solving crimes. Each title in the series demonstrates the ways a crime may be solved, from the various applications of forensic science and technology to the reasoning of investigators. Sidebars examine both the limits and possibilities of the new technologies and present crime statistics, career information, and step-by-step explanations of scientific and legal processes.

The Crime Scene Investigations series strives to be both informative and realistic about how members of law enforcement—criminal investigators, forensic scientists, and others—solve crimes, for it is essential that student researchers understand that crime solving is rarely quick or easy. Many factors—from a detective's dogged pursuit of one tenuous lead to a suspect's careless mistakes to sheer luck to complex calculations computed in the lab—are all part of crime solving today.

The Science of Making and Breaking Codes

Writing is a part of most people's everyday life, whether they are jotting down grocery lists or composing a paper for an English class, sending a text message or posting a blog. They write to communicate with others and to remember things. Some written material, such as a diary, is meant to be completely private. Other writing, such as a love letter, may be meant for one person only. Throughout history, humans have gone to extraordinary measures to hide their private messages from spying eyes. Diaries have locks, for example, and, even then, they are usually stored somewhere secret because the breach of their contents could mean humiliation for the author. Other written information is so important that if it fell into the wrong hands, it could result in loss of money, freedom, or even human life. In a case like this, the text of a communication is often disguised to guarantee that even if the message were stolen, no one but the author and the intended recipient would be able to read it. The need to mask writing from unintended readers gave rise to cryptology, the study and practice of writing in codes and ciphers.

Cryptology methods have existed for thousands of years. War generals during the time of the ancient Greeks and Romans made some of the earliest attempts to conceal messages. They needed to send messages across battlefields to coordinate their war plans, so they made their writing unintelligible to any opponent who might intercept it. They used code words to stand for real words, jumbled the letters of their messages, and invented ciphers, which replaced each letter of a written message with a different letter or symbol. Unfortunately, the cleverness of people masking the messages was almost always matched by

the cleverness of people who were skilled at *unmasking* them. These are the two distinct sides to cryptology: cryptography, the writing of disguised messages, and cryptanalysis, the cracking of the codes or ciphers used during cryptography to reveal the original message.

In war and also in crime, cryptology has often been a linchpin to success. An unbreakable code could be behind an unbeatable army or an unsolvable criminal deed, but the breaking of a code often leads to defeat for armies and criminals alike. The trickier cryptographers become with their methods, the more inventive cryptanalysts are at finding solutions. Cryptology advances as cryptographers and cryptanalysts each try to stay a step ahead of the other. In modern times the field of cryptology has branched out into computerized methods that create the most secure ciphers cryptology has ever seen, but those who practice this science realize there has never been and may never be a code that is completely impossible to break.

Although there may never be a code that is completely impossible to break, modern cryptology keeps online shoppers and bankers safe from criminals.

9

Forensic cryptologists are code and cipher experts who protect law-abiding citizens from criminal cryptographers and cryptanalysts. They are the forensic specialists who analyze criminals' encoded plans and also create methods for citizens to protect their own information from criminals' prying eyes. Today's forensic cryptologists find themselves deep in the secret communications of gangsters and drug lords, smugglers and murderers, spies and terrorists. Lives and livelihoods are at stake, and both may depend on the ability of forensic cryptologists to uncover and read the message beneath the disguise.

CHAPTER 1

What is Cryptology?

The practice of writing, or giving a picture of human thought in symbols for the purpose of communication, has existed for tens of thousands of years. In the Stone Age, human beings on every continent developed forms of writing to represent and preserve spoken stories. Some of the earliest writing took the form of pictures and symbols carved into or painted on cave walls and rocks. This writing often told the stories of warriors and other important people. Where examples of these early attempts at writing still exist, they give important clues about the ancient cultures that created them.

In time, writing did more than tell stories in pictures. It became a way to communicate directly with other people. Eventually, writing became portable. The ancient Sumerians, for example, learned to carve symbols into small pieces of clay that they used as coins, handing them back and forth as a means of currency. Long passages of writing were carved into clay tablets in Mesopotamia. Ancient Egyptians learned to use ink and to write on strips of paper made from papyrus plants that they could then hand to other people. The ability to pass written messages back and forth, or for messengers to carry them from one group of people to another, was an important step for civilization. The leaders of different groups could communicate from a distance, and this helped bring small groups of people together into larger communities. "Mesopotamian city-states grew into powerful empires once complete writing had emerged in that region," says Steven Roger Fischer, director of the Institute of Polynesian Languages and Literatures in Auckland, New Zealand. "More societies borrowed and adapted the wonder of this new form of writing."[1] With the help of written communication, modern civilizations were born.

Once writing became widespread, people saw a need to mask it for privacy and secrecy. Written messages were vulnerable. If they were intercepted and read on the way from the author to the recipient, someone else would know the secrets. To keep important messages private, civilizations invented ways of disguising their writing so that only the intended recipients could understand it. Methods of masking and unmasking written messages have been around almost as long as writing itself.

Hidden Messages

The need to hide messages arises because information has value. In modern times people carefully guard their bank account information from potential thieves, for example. Food manufacturers closely guard their secret recipes. Teachers forbid students from sharing written information during class tests. It is human nature to keep important information a secret, and, when the information exists in written form, people devise ways to disguise the information so that no one can read it without permission from the writer. The practice of disguising written messages is called "cryptography," from the Greek word *kryptos*, meaning "hidden," and *graph*, meaning "write."

Techniques of secret writing date back at least to the time of the ancient Egyptians, who at first experimented with cryptology just to see if it could be done. "It was more of a game than anything else...just a puzzle," says cryptology expert David Kahn about the Egyptians' attempts to disguise various symbols of text. They also used cryptology for a real and very important purpose—disguising the complex instructions for their sacred methods of mummifying the dead. The Egyptians' masked hieroglyphs included both of the elements central to cryptography: the goal of secrecy and the transformation of letters to make words seem like nonsense. "And so," Kahn says, "cryptology was born."[2]

Cryptography, or writing masked messages, may have begun as a game among the Egyptians, but the ancient Greeks devised their own methods as a matter of military necessity.

1		2		3		4		5	
α	*1*	ζ	*1*	λ	*1*	π	*1*	φ	*1*
β	*2*	η	*2*	μ	*2*	ϱ	*2*	χ	*2*
γ	*3*	θ	*3*	ν	*3*	σ	*3*	ψ	*3*
δ	*4*	ι	*4*	ξ	*4*	τ	*4*	ω	*4*
ε	*5*	ϰ	*5*	ο	*5*	υ	*5*		

The ancient Greeks devised methods of cryptography as a way to communicate secretly during wartime. For example, the Polybius Square, developed by Greek scholar Polybius, replaces each letter of the Greek alphabet with a pair of numbers.

The Spartans, a Greek civilization known for warfare and military tactics, understood that it was vital to guard written messages sent between their generals during battle, because if these messages were stolen and read by spies, the enemy would know their war strategies and plans, and entire battles could be lost. Thus, Greek generals devised various methods of cryptography to pass private messages to each other during wartime. "The world owes its first instructional text on communications security to the Greeks,"[3] says Kahn. The subject took up an entire chapter in one of the earliest known works on military science, *On the Defense of Fortified Places*, by Greek author Aeneas the Tactician. One method required a device called the "skytale," a wooden staff or pole around which the author of a message wrapped a long strip of leather or parchment before writing the message down the length of the staff. When the parchment was unwound, it could be carried, safely unreadable, to its destination. Only when the intended recipient, who had a staff of exactly the same thickness, wound the strip around his own skytale would the message be readable.

Like the Greeks, the ancient Romans invented various methods of secret writing for use in battle, but they took cryptography a step further. Whereas Greek methods such as the skytale required an object for decoding that could fall into enemy hands, the Romans devised a different way to mask messages from anyone but the intended reader: they wrote their messages in codes and ciphers. A code is a cryptographic method that replaces entire words or phrases with other words (*sword* might be changed to the codeword *apple*, for example, and the codeword *dance* might stand for the phrase *head to the west*). A cipher is a method that replaces each individual letter of a message with a different letter, number, or symbol (every *a* is changed to something else, then every *b*, and so on). Once the Romans had disguised a plaintext—an original, unmasked message—with codes or ciphers, it was difficult or impossible for anyone to understand the message unless he knew the key—the list of which words, letters, or symbols had been used to mask the original message. Only then could the recipient reverse the cryptography process and transform the writing back to its original plaintext version.

The invention of codes and ciphers made it possible to send any number of masked messages to other people and even send messages to different recipients using different codes and

The blackboard displays the popular Caesar cipher, which replaces plaintext letters with letters standing three places further down in the alphabet.

ciphers with different keys. The Roman emperor Julius Caesar was especially fond of cryptology and invented a now-famous cipher that replaced each letter of the original message with a letter a few places further along in the alphabet: every *a* in the original message became a *d*, for example, every *b* became an *e*, and so forth. "To this day," says Kahn, "any cipher that

Solving a Simple Cipher

One type of cipher is a cryptogram, a puzzle in which each alphabet letter is replaced with a different one. Professional cryptanalysts usually solve ciphers far more difficult than simple cryptograms, but the general methods used are the same:

1 Write the alphabet in a line so you can write the replacement letters (the key) alongside as you figure them out.

2 Look for single-letter words; in English, these are usually "I" or "a."

3 Remember that every word has at least one vowel, so look for two-letter groups and try combinations such as *if*, *is*, *at*, and *to*.

4 Look for a reappearing three-letter group. It is probably *the*. If this seems to work in the puzzle, fill in *t*, *h*, and *e* in the key.

5 Look for double letters. At the ends of words, these are usually *ll* or *ss*. In the middle of words, they may be *ee* or *oo*.

6 When stumped, make educated guesses, discarding any that cannot work (for example, if you know *k* already, it is not likely to be followed by a *d*).

7 Fill in letter substitutions as you figure them out. The message will gradually reveal itself.

consists of a standard sequence ... in which the plaintext letters were replaced by letters standing three places further down the alphabet ... is called a Caesar alphabet."[4]

Breaking Codes

Along with methods for disguising written messages came the need for unintended readers to unmask them. Just as it was important for warring armies to communicate their battle plans with one another in secret, it was important for the opposing sides to try to intercept these important messages and make sense of them. The process of cryptography, or re-writing messages in ciphers or codes, is also called "encryption." Its opposite, "decryption," means using the key to work backwards and transform an encoded message back to its original, plaintext version. Decryption, although often tedious and time-consuming, is usually a simple

A Noble Cipher

Civil war afflicted England in the 1600s. Some people thought the king, Charles I, should have complete power over the country. Others wanted to put limits on the king's power. The two sides went to war in 1642. Sir John Trevanion, a nobleman who supported the king, was captured by the king's opponents and imprisoned in a castle to await almost certain execution. One night Trevanion's jailer handed him a letter from his servant. Trevanion's captors had carefully examined the letter, but found no information that could help him. When Trevanion studied the letter closely, however, he discovered that it did contain a hidden message, a cipher made from every third letter after a punctuation mark. When Trevanion put these letters together, they spelled out a lifesaving phrase: *panel at east end of chapel slides*. Trevanion later asked his captors if he could spend some time alone in the chapel to pray. They granted his request. When they came back for him, he was gone.

and straightforward process of changing each word or letter back to its original form. But when messages are intercepted by unauthorized people who do not have a key, they must figure out what encryption process was used so they can decrypt messages without the cryptographer's knowledge. Solving codes and ciphers without knowing the key is called "cryptanalysis." It can be very challenging and can take a lot of time, but persistent cryptanalysts know that any code or cipher can be broken eventually. "Cryptography and cryptanalysis are

By the Numbers

45,000

Approximate number of enciphered enemy telegrams cryptanalyzed by the U.S. military during World War I

the two faces of cryptology," says mathematics and computer science professor Freidrich Ludwig Bauer. "Each depends on the other and each influences the other in an interplay of improvements to strengthen cryptanalytic security on the one side and efforts to mount more efficient attacks on the other side."[5]

Cryptology in the Civil War

The struggle between cryptography and cryptanalysis has affected national security throughout history, determining the outcomes of battles not only among ancient Romans and Greeks but in modern wars as well. In the United States in the 1860s, cryptology was a factor in the outcome of the Civil War that broke out between states of the Union in the North, who wanted to keep the United States together, and states of the Confederacy in the South, who wanted to secede from the Union and become a separate nation. The war raged across American soil for four years, but the Union had advantages in technology that the Confederacy lacked. Its superior railway system, for one, made it possible for trains to carry supplies to Union soldiers, who were therefore better equipped than the Confederates. The Union had another technological advantage: an intricate network of wooden poles and wires strung across the countryside for long-distance communication by a recent invention called the telegraph.

THE ARMY TELEGRAPH—SETTING UP THE WIRE DURING AN ACTION.—[Sketched by Mr. A. R. Waud.]

During the U.S. Civil War, the Union Army used cryptology to send wartime telegraph messages in cipher.

"American wars had always been fought with the head of government removed from the scene of battle," says historian Tom Wheeler, former president and chairman of the Foundation for the National Archives. "[President] Lincoln used the telegraph. ... to propel his leadership vision to the front."[6] Lincoln made sure that his Union Army had the best and latest in communication methods. "The immediacy of electronic messages put the president in his general's tent, capable of a rapid-fire back-and-forth exchange almost as if he were physically present,"[7] Wheeler says. The enemy could easily intercept telegraph messages, however, so to disguise them, the Union Army used cryptology and sent its wartime telegrams in cipher. "In order to deceive the Confederate operator," said David Homer Bates, one of three cryptologists in the Union Army and the manager of the War Department Telegraph Office during the Civil War, "we sent ... a number of cipher messages, easy of translation, and which contained all sorts of bogus information for misleading the enemy."[8] Meanwhile, Union cryptologists also intercepted messages from the Confederates. They were using cryptology too, but Confederate ciphers were not nearly as advanced as those of the Union. "They were generally ordinary letter ciphers, the letters of the alphabet being transformed in various ways," said Bates. "As a rule, we were able to translate these ciphers."[9]

Although the Confederate Army attempted to disguise its telegraph messages in codes, it had an unorganized system for doing so. Different commanders used different methods for their codes and ciphers, as opposed to the Union, which had a more consistent system. Many Confederate cryptographers also did a poor job of encoding or enciphering their messages. Kahn says one Confederate general's cryptologists tried for twelve hours to make sense of a garbled message. The general "finally gave up in disgust and galloped around the Union flank to the sender to find out what it said."[10] The Union's superior method for disguising its own messages and for reading the encrypted messages of the Confederacy was one of its best weapons. Cryptology played an important role in the Union's victory during the Civil War, and the war in turn led to important innovations in the science of cryptology.

Cryptology in Modern Wars

In the twentieth century, wars again played out beneath the cloak of secret writing, this time on a worldwide scale in battles that spanned oceans. The outcome of both World Wars in the 1900s depended in great part on the ability of the Allied nations—those who sided with the United States and Great Britain—to exchange encoded information with each other and their armed forces to carry out battle preparations in secret. At the same time the Allies needed to make sense of their enemies' coded communications to learn what those nations were planning. World War II, especially, became a war of cryptology.

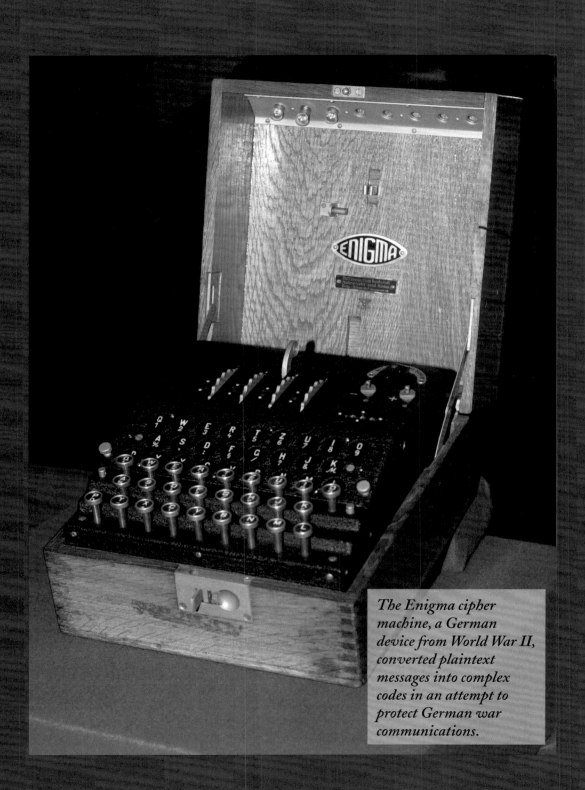

The Enigma cipher machine, a German device from World War II, converted plaintext messages into complex codes in an attempt to protect German war communications.

The Axis powers—Germany, Japan, and Italy, who were enemies of the Allies—were skilled at encoding information to make it unreadable to anyone but the intended recipients. Complex encoded messages were sent over radio airwaves by the thousands. The Germans had invented a machine, called the ENIGMA, that converted plaintext messages into extremely complicated ciphers. The Japanese had an enciphering process of their own, which U.S. cryptologists called PURPLE. Cryptologists in Great Britain and the United States worked feverishly throughout the war to decode German and Japanese communications without letting their enemies realize it was happening. The ability to do this gave the Allies a tremendous advantage in the war. They could spy on their enemies and predict the next wartime moves. Methods of cryptology, says Bauer, "are weapons for defense and weapons for attack. The Second World War ... taught us this lesson."[11]

> **By the Numbers**
>
> # 158 QUIN-TILLION
>
> **Number of different ways Germany's World War II coding machine, the ENIGMA, could encode a message**

The work of American and British cryptologists during World War II was so vital to the outcome of the war that they carried it out in extremely secretive ways. If Germany and Japan figured out that the Allies were breaking their codes, they would change their encryption methods, making their codes and ciphers even more difficult to solve. Secrecy was therefore critical, as is often the case with cryptology. In the United States and in Britain, cryptologists were sworn to confidentiality and often worked in locations undisclosed to the public as they decoded message after message and passed these enemy communications on to government and military officials. Working together, American and British cryptologists undermined the cryptographic efforts of their enemies as they uncovered the secret messages and plans of the Axis powers. As Bauer notes, "once cryptological information is disclosed, a government's interest in protecting national security is damaged and may

Unsung Heroes

During World War II, the U.S. military solved many encrypted German and Japanese messages, but the Japanese attempted to decrypt American messages, too. The United States needed an encoding system its enemies could not break. In 1942 a group of Navajo joined the U.S. military and formed the Navajo Code Talker unit, devising a complex, spoken code made entirely of words

The Navajo Code Talker unit, formed during World War II, devised a complicated spoken code made entirely from words of the native Navajo language. The code proved unbreakable.

from their native language. Every member of the unit had to memorize the code; they were forbidden to write any of it down. During many major battles of World War II, Navajo Code Talkers communicated by radio in a code that no eavesdropper in the world could understand. They could say in seconds what took coding machines an hour or more to encrypt. Their code proved completely unbreakable and helped the U.S. win major victories such as the battle for the Japanese island of Iwo Jima in 1945.

After the war the Navajo Code Talkers went home without fanfare. The government classified their achievements, and for decades no one knew what this group of Native Americans had accomplished for their country. Finally, in 2001 the Navajo Code Talkers were given Congressional Medals of Honor, the highest award an American soldier can receive.

not be repaired."[12] Such was the case for the Axis governments in World War II. Largely due to the work of cryptologists, the Allied powers, led by the U.S. and Great Britain, eventually won the war.

Cryptology and Crime

Cryptology's role in national defense may be one of its most honorable uses. Throughout its history, however, the science of cryptology has been tainted by dishonest motives. In the Middle Ages, secret writing was often used to disguise magical spells, curses, and chemical formulas for potions. Cryptology has also been one of the main tools of spies through history. Even in World War II, the methods by which the Allies intercepted and analyzed their enemies' secret messages could be considered sneaky and dishonest, despite being so important to the outcome of the war. Cryptology has gained a dirty reputation over the centuries, one that has not been helped by the fact that it has a longstanding role in the history of crime.

Criminals, for whom sneakiness and dishonesty are a way of life, have long capitalized on the practice of secret writing to help them hide their plans and carry out their various misdeeds. But wherever there are cryptographers, there are also cryptanalysts, and this has led to a field in crime science called "forensic cryptology," or the study of secret messages used to commit crime. "Cryptology...has points of contact with criminology," says Bauer, "usually accompanied by successfully cryptanalyzed secret messages from criminals still at large—smugglers, drug dealers, gun-runners, blackmailers, or swindlers—and some already behind bars."[13] Indeed, one of the most famous historical examples of the criminal use of cryptology involved a notorious woman who was already under arrest.

A Code for Treason

In the sixteenth century, Elizabeth I was queen of England, and Mary, Queen of Scots, was next in line to inherit the throne. Mary developed elaborate plans to have Elizabeth assassinated

Mary, Queen of Scots, next in line to inherit the English throne, plotted to kill Elizabeth I, the queen of England. Mary communicated with conspirators using enciphered notes.

so that she herself would become queen. Elizabeth was aware of Mary's intentions and kept Mary under house arrest in a castle where she could be closely watched. Communication with outsiders was forbidden. Mary needed a way to contact her conspirators, the partners in her scheme, so she used beer kegs to smuggle written messages in and out of the castle. Because she was plotting to kill the queen, a crime punishable by death, it was very important to Mary that only the intended recipients of her messages would be able to read them. She had her personal secretary encipher all of her notes, using different ciphers for different recipients. She also demanded that the enciphering methods be changed frequently in case her enemies solved one method.

A messenger Mary trusted to carry her encrypted messages to her allies eventually betrayed her. The messenger instead turned the notes over to one of Queen Elizabeth's law enforcement officials, who for months collected Mary's notes and had them deciphered. Criminal evidence of treason, in the form of cryptographic correspondence, piled up against Mary and her conspirators. At her trial Mary's notes and the cipher alphabets she had used to disguise them were used as proof of her guilt in plotting the murder of Queen Elizabeth. Mary was convicted of high treason and was executed on February 8, 1587. Her case is one of the most famous examples in history of cryptology's being used to convict someone of a crime. "There seems little doubt that [Mary] would have died before her time, the politics of the day being what they were," says Kahn. "But there seems equally little doubt that cryptology hastened her unnatural end."[14]

An Infamous Assassination

Three hundred years after cryptology brought about the downfall of Mary, Queen of Scots, it was used in a criminal plot against the life of another prominent leader. The assassin was loyal to the Confederacy that had just lost the American Civil War, and the target of the murder was Abraham Lincoln, president of the United States and himself a great pioneer of cryptologic technology.

Lafayette Baker, Chief of Intelligence for the Union during the U.S. Civil War, wrote coded messages that seemed to accuse many people of playing a role in Abraham Lincoln's assassination.

The assassination of Lincoln was carried out by John Wilkes Booth, who sneaked into Ford's Theater in Washington, D.C., on the evening of April 15, 1865, and shot the president in the head. Booth escaped from the theater but was tracked by law enforcement officers across the country to a farm in Virginia, where he was shot and killed on April 26. Booth had not acted alone to assassinate the president, however. Evidence collected from the hotel room he had stayed in before the assassination included a note written in cipher. This suggested that Booth had conspirators in the crime, and that they had communicated in code. Trial lawyers said that the cipher found in Booth's room had been encoded by the same cipher machine the Confederate leader, Jefferson Davis, used to communicate with his own secret agents. Lawyers during the trial questioned how the cipher ended up among Booth's belongings: "Who gave Booth the cipher? Of what use was it to him if he was not in confederation with Davis?"[15] In the end the origin of the cipher remained a mystery, but eight people accused of having a part in Lincoln's murder were tried and found guilty in July 1865. Four were sent to prison, and the other four were hanged. Davis was not among them. He was never charged with conspiracy to assassinate his worst enemy, Abraham Lincoln, but because of the cipher, rumors of his possible involvement in the crime exist to this day.

The conspiracy theories surrounding Lincoln's murder did not end with the 1865 trial. In the 1960s hidden coded messages were found in documents that had belonged to Lafayette Baker, Chief of Intelligence for the Union during the Civil War. Baker's messages, when deciphered, seemed to accuse many people of having roles in the Lincoln assassination plot, including Edwin M. Stanton, who had served as Secretary of War during the Civil War, and possibly even Lincoln's vice president, Andrew Johnson. According to many sources, Baker was not an honest man, and this cast doubt on his encrypted accusations. "Did Lafayette Baker tell the truth," asks historian John Chandler Griffin, "or was he merely trying to settle an old score with Stanton?"[16]

The accusations Baker encoded in the 1860s may have been a hoax, but the interest they have created among modern-day historians shows the influence that coded messages have on people's perceptions of crime. Cryptology's ties to secret messages and criminal activity throughout history have given it a notorious reputation. "During all these years, cryptology was acquiring a taint that lingers even today—the conviction in the minds of many people that cryptology is a black art,"[17] says Kahn. To this day, many criminals collaborate in code, and police often need cryptology to catch them.

CHAPTER 2

How Criminals Use Cryptology

A delicate balance has always existed between criminals and the investigators who want to outwit them. People who commit crimes try to hide what they are doing or what they have done, and people who solve crimes try to reveal what illegal activity has taken place and who did it. Criminals who successfully veil the planning of their crimes usually remain uncaught, and, because cryptology is one of the best ways to disguise criminal plans, it has a long history as a tool used in crime. Whether criminals are captured or remain free often depends on the cryptanalysis skills of investigators who have the job of intercepting and reading disguised criminal communications. The messages they decode come from all kinds of criminals. Murderers, thieves, and spies have all used cryptology, and it is especially popular among crooks who smuggle illegal substances. Such criminals have created some of the most formidable challenges in the history of forensic investigation. Cryptologists help put a stop to their crime sprees.

A Setup for Smuggling

In the years between the American Civil War and World War I, alcohol became a villain in the opinion of many Americans. By the end of World War I in 1918, more than a hundred thousand saloons were in business across the United States, and public drunkenness was a widespread problem. People blamed liquor for a rise in violent crime, prostitution, and other social blights, so individual states banned saloons and alcohol manufacturing inside their borders. This anti-liquor trend swept across the nation, and in 1919 Congress approved the Eighteenth Amendment to the U.S. Constitution, forbidding the making, selling, or transportation of liquor anywhere in the United States. The new policy was called "Prohibition."

The National Prohibition Act allowed police to enforce the no-drinking rules of the Eighteenth Amendment by searching citizens and their homes for liquor and arresting people who made or kept alcohol. Enforcement was no easy task, however. The public's demand for liquor only grew stronger once the substance had been banned, and criminals saw an opportunity to make a lot of money from liquor-seeking citizens. These crooks had no objection to breaking Prohibition laws to make booze or smuggle it into the United States from countries where liquor was still legal. "The popular demand for liquor made it sufficiently profitable to outweigh the legal risks,"[18] says history professor James Klein.

Prohibition led to a notorious new trend of lawbreaking: organized crime. Gangs of wealthy and powerful criminals, known as "mobsters," banded together in the 1920s to organize and operate illegal saloons called "speakeasies." Smuggling alcohol became a prosperous enterprise. To evade police, the organized crime network needed a form of secretive communication to supply their speakeasy customers with a steady stream of alcohol. Thus, Prohibition brought about one of the most successful stints of secret criminal communication that cryptology has ever known.

Rumrunning in Code

Mobsters who ran speakeasies had large networks of criminal employees they paid to supply them with liquor. There were two types of smugglers. Those who worked on land to bring liquor directly to the speakeasies became known as bootleggers, because bottles of booze were often hidden under pant legs or in boots. Those who worked the seas to bring in shipments of liquor from foreign countries were called rumrunners. The rumrunners quickly became the government's leading target for stopping the smuggling of liquor during Prohibition, because if booze was not crossing the nation's borders to begin with, there would be far fewer bootleggers and secret speakeasies on land.

Only with the help of an expert cryptologist was the U.S. Coast Guard able to crack the secret communications used by rumrunners who were transporting barrels of illegal alcohol into U.S. harbors.

The United States Coast Guard was charged with keeping rumrunners out, but the seafaring smugglers outsmarted law enforcement officers again and again. They communicated by radio messages, which the Coast Guard easily intercepted, but the messages themselves were disguised in codes and cipher systems that were even more complex than methods the world governments had used during World War I. "Practically every rum boat on the Pacific Coast had its own code or cipher," says David Kahn. One off-shore liquor supplier, he says, "employed a different cryptosystem from its headquarters to each of its 'blacks,' or rumrunning craft."[19] The illegal alcohol trade was both powerful and profitable, and organized crime rings could afford to invest large sums of money into their cryptology efforts. "It was reported that one syndicate paid its radio expert $10,000 a year," says Kahn. "This during the Depression!... His name was unknown, but his cryptologic expertise was apparent. The smugglers' systems grew increasingly more complicated."[20] The variety and complexity of their cryptography methods made the rumrunners' communications seem impossible to crack. They easily evaded the Coast Guard and dropped their shipments of booze at secret locations on shore.

The Coast Guard needed a cryptologist of its own, one whose skills were a match for the rumrunners and their ciphers. The government turned to one of the country's best cryptologists, a woman named Elizebeth Friedman. Friedman was a skilled codebreaker who had worked for the U.S. Army, Navy, and State Department during World War I. When the Coast Guard hired her to help crack the codes of the rumrunners, she said the systems the criminals used were among the greatest code-breaking challenges of her career. "Some of these are of a complexity never even attempted by any government for its most secret communications," she wrote in a report in 1930. "At no time during the World War, when secret methods of communication reached their highest development, were there used such involved ramifications as are to be found in some of the correspondence of West Coast rum running vessels."[21]

Despite the challenge they presented, Friedman was able to cryptanalyze the rumrunners' complicated encryption methods, and law enforcement officers were finally able to understand the messages and apprehend rumrunners before they got their shipments of liquor to shore. The Coast Guard's success at stopping rumrunners during Prohibition depended almost entirely on its cryptanalytic unit, which consisted of only two people, Friedman and her clerk. Despite the fact that she worked alone, Friedman's code-breaking skills helped stop the widespread crime of some of the most notorious smugglers in U.S. history. "Neither before nor since have criminals ever used such extensive and complicated systems of secret writing," says Kahn. Friedman "crowned this work with solutions of messages that helped destroy one of the largest smuggling rings in the United States."[22]

The era of Prohibition came to an end on December 5, 1933, when Congress passed the Twenty-first Amendment to repeal the Eighteenth Amendment. The ban on liquor, which had been enforced for a decade and a half, came to an end, and the possession, use, and sale of alcohol became legal in the U.S.

Secrets Under Cover

Disguising messages using ciphers is a means of *overt*, or obvious, secret writing—it is apparent that the message exists and has been disguised. Sometimes, the very existence of a secret message is hidden. This practice of creating *covert*, or concealed, secret writing is called steganography.

Many clever methods of steganography have been used. For example, classical composer Johann Sebastian Bach disguised signatures, parts of his own name and the names of fellow musicians, in the notes of some of his music. Hollow coins have been used to enclose information, and invisible ink has a long history as well. Spies hide messages within books by placing tiny, almost imperceptible, marks over certain letters; when the recipient of the book places these letters in order, they spell a message. A microdot is an image or a passage of text that is photographed and then reduced to the size of the period at the end of this sentence, hiding a message from any who do not know to enlarge it. Modern steganographers embed information into digital image files, invisible to the naked eye. Often used together with cryptography, steganography is a popular way to mask a written secret.

once again. The end of Prohibition also marked the end of a profitable criminal alcohol trade. It did not, however, bring about the end of organized crime, or of smuggling. Alcohol was legalized, but other substances—namely drugs—were not. In the decades that followed Prohibition, drugs replaced alcohol as a leading commodity of organized crime. Today's police forces cope constantly with the smuggling and trade of illegal drugs, much as law enforcement officers of the Prohibition era coped with bootleggers and rumrunners. Organized crime in the form of gangs is still a big business in the criminal underworld, and communicating in code has not gone out of style. "Criminals have always needed to keep secrets," says Daniel Olson, a forensic cryptologist with the Federal Bureau of Investigation (FBI). "As technology increases, criminals will continue to find new ways to communicate."[23]

Codes of the Drug Trade

In the decades that followed Prohibition, drugs took the place of alcohol as the illegal substance people blamed for many of society's ills. The Controlled Substances Act, passed in 1970, outlawed the possession, use, and sale of harmful and addicting drugs, including heroin, cocaine, marijuana, LSD, and many others. It also forbade drug-related "writing,

Modern drug dealers use various forms of cryptology as a way to mask their involvement in the drug trade.

signs, signals, pictures, or sounds" in any kind of public messages, including "mail, telephone, wire, radio, and all other means of communication."[24] Since it is illegal to communicate in any way about drug-related business, today's drug dealers have turned to various forms of cryptology to disguise their messages and mask their involvement in the drug trade. Unlike the complex cipher systems used by smugglers during Prohibition, much of the communication in the drug business of today takes the form of simple codes and numbers that are quickly transmitted using the latest forms of communication technology. The National Drug Intelligence Center says that "distributors use cell phones, satellite phones, pagers, and other personal communication devices to communicate with sources and customers. In addition, distributors often use text messages consisting of code words that allow them to communicate with a reduced risk of detection."[25]

Drug dealers use encoded text messages and pager messages to reveal drug-related information quickly, efficiently, and secretly. The number thirteen, for example, is often typed to indicate the thirteenth letter of the alphabet, *M*, which usually stands for marijuana or methamphetamine. Olson says that common messages pertaining to drug deals "normally consist of dates, accounts, units, prices, and sometimes drug types."[26] For example, he says, the code *772 111* could indicate that customer #772 is asking about the price for one ounce (28g) of cocaine. "Codes are typically used to add two elements to communications: secrecy and brevity," says Olson. "Criminals use codes for both purposes."[27] For drug dealers, codes provide secrecy, because innocent bystanders who happen to glance at a cell phone or pager and see these numbers will not realize that a drug sale is being organized. Codes are also efficient because by typing just six numbers, a potential customer is able to communicate a lot of information to a drug dealer. This makes codes a very common and attractive form of communication in the trade of illegal drugs.

Drug dealers mask their criminal occupation in spoken conversations, not just text-based ones, to avoid arousing suspicion among bystanders who overhear them. "Typically

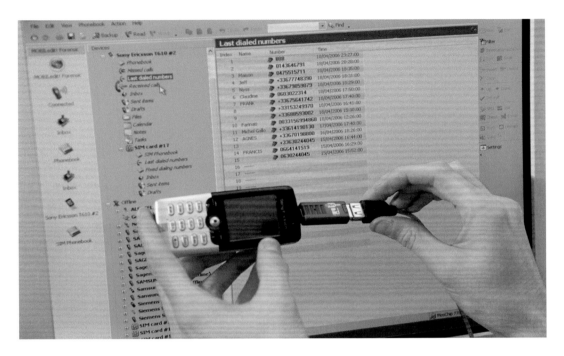

different codewords are used in conversation to differentiate between drug types," says Olson. "For example, the code white indicates cocaine, and green indicates marijuana. Drug traffickers often use codewords to disguise their activity, and these are limited only by the imagination of the drug trafficker."[28] Understanding codes like these requires little cryptologic science, because codes replace entire words or phrases with other words instead of changing the individual letters of the written message the way ciphers do. As long as one knows what words the codes stand for, he or she can easily understand an encoded message. Drug dealers and traffickers change their codes all the time, however. The main challenge for cryptologists is keeping track of the changing codes. "Unlike cipher systems which can be deciphered using set procedures and techniques, codes cannot be deciphered without some knowledge of what the writer is attempting to conceal,"[29] Olson says. Because drug dealers and other criminals do not readily share this information with police, codes are a very useful tool for criminals and a challenge even for investigators with training in cryptology.

Drug distributors often use coded text messages to communicate with suppliers and customers.

Graffiti as Cryptography

Not all criminals who use codes do so to conceal their communication. Some encoded messages having to do with crime are not hidden in any way, but are meant for the world to see. Graffiti is a prominent example in the modern world. An illegal activity in itself, graffiti is nevertheless used frequently by criminals, especially gangs, as a form of encrypted, but very public, communication.

Graffiti is the act of drawing, writing, or scribbling on a public surface such as a wall. It is not a new idea; ancient Romans carved graffiti marks into the architecture at Pompeii before the city was destroyed by a volcanic eruption in A.D.79, and some of these are still visible in the city's surviving ruins. In the early 1900s homeless vagrants and tramps who traveled the U.S. by train and begged door to door at people's homes and businesses used graffiti. They marked buildings and sites with graffiti messages to communicate to one another, and graffiti symbols represented many things, including "town is hostile," "stay away," "good for a handout," and "plainclothes detectives here."

In the past few decades, however, graffiti has become larger, more colorful, and a more rampant social problem. It covers walls, buildings, billboards, and businesses, especially in large cities, and it is one of the main methods of communication between street gangs who use codes and symbols in graffiti to

In the 1930s, during the Great Depression, traveling homeless people used symbols to communicate to one another. For example, the symbols pictured mean: "leave town," "safe camp," and "judge."

Leave Town

Safe Camp

Judge

make statements to members of their own and other groups. "Communities that produce graffiti … may target cryptic messages toward their own closed community, producing a seemingly confusing and unreadable product,"[30] says Susan Phillips, a photographer and anthropologist who studies street gangs. Gang graffiti consists of symbols, icons, and encoded messages that are visible to everyone but only make sense to people affiliated with gangs and who understand the code. Gangs spray-paint their own symbols and icons on walls of buildings and other surfaces to mark territory, for example, but they also paint the symbols that stand for their rivals, often splitting the symbols in half or writing portions of words or symbols upside down and backwards to communicate disrespect, anger, or violent intentions toward other gangs.

Although gang graffiti is very public, the actual message is meant to be understood only by other gang members.

"Graffiti warns intruders or trespassers from rival gangs, and even policemen, that they are not welcome," says Robert Walker, a former federal law enforcement officer who now leads workshops on gang awareness for police departments around the country. "It may also be an advertisement for the sale of drugs or a memorial to a fallen fellow gang member." Walker calls graffiti "the newspaper, the billboard, the Internet of the world of street gangs," and although not all graffiti is gang-related, Walker says it is "often the first indication that street gangs are active in your community."[31] Graffiti is a constant concern for police, not only because it is vandalism but because it often encodes communication between criminals who are planning crimes ranging from drug trafficking to murder. The ability to read the information encoded in graffiti has become an important application of forensic cryptology in recent decades.

Cipher of a Killer

Gangs are not the only criminals who communicate publicly in code about their illegal activity. Even criminals who act independently sometimes use encrypted communication to brag about their crimes and their ability to get away with what they have done. They seem to take pride in their cryptologic craftiness. One of the most notorious serial killers of the past century had a fascination for communicating with the police in codes and ciphers, and he left an unforgettable mark on the field of forensic cryptology. On October 30, 1966, this killer claimed his first victim, a college freshman named Cheri Jo Bates. She was murdered near a parking lot outside the library of Riverside College in southern California, and police in the area received a letter a few days later stating details of the crime that only the investigators and the person who committed the murder could have known. The letter included a warning: "She is not the first and she will not be the last … I am insane. But that will not stop the game."[32]

For six months, no other letters came from the killer. Then Riverside's local newspaper, the *Riverside Press-Enterprise*, printed an article about Bates' murder, which was still unsolved. A day later, handwritten letters were mailed to the newspaper, the Riverside police, and Bates' father, stating that Bates "had to die" and threatening that "there will be more."[33] The letter was signed with what looked like the letter *Z*. Police in Riverside and the surrounding communities, believing a serial killer could be on the loose, braced for more murders. But for a year and a half, no more correspondence came to them or the newspaper from the mysterious *Z*, and no murders were linked to the killer.

Then, on December 20, 1968, two teenagers were shot and killed near their parked car at a reservoir outside of Vallejo, California, just north of the San Francisco Bay. Six months later, on July 4, 1969, another young couple in a parked car was attacked by a shooter only two miles from the murder site of the first couple. The crimes were so similar that police suspected they had been committed by the same person. This suspicion was confirmed when *Z* sent letters to the editors of three newspapers in the area: the *Vallejo Times-Herald*, the *San Francisco Examiner*, and the *San Francisco Chronicle*. The author claimed he was the shooter in the recent killings, again giving details of the crime that only the investigators and the killer could have known. Each of the letters also contained a third of a message written in cipher. *Z* gave instructions to each of the newspapers to print their portion of the cipher on their front page on August 1, or, he warned, he would go on a killing rampage. He also promised that the cipher, solved

Pictured is a portion of a cipher message sent by the Zodiac Killer that was decoded by high school teacher Donald Harden and his wife.

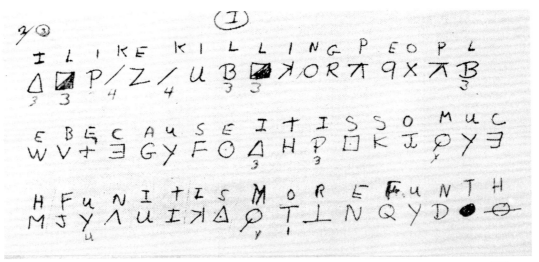

39

By the Numbers

340

Total number of symbols in the cipher the Zodiac Killer sent to San Francisco newspapers in 1969

correctly, would reveal his identity. All three newspapers printed their portion of the cipher message. Each of the three parts was eight lines long, written in a simple substitution cipher that replaced the actual letters of the message with symbols. On August 4, Don Harden, a Salinas, California, schoolteacher, and his wife solved the cipher.

"The Harden decoding was confirmed by Naval Intelligence," says true-crime author Brian Innes. *Z*'s cipher was not as clever as he probably intended it to be. "It's apparent that, even with the substitution table at his side, the killer made several errors."[34] The solved cipher message was poorly written and riddled with misspellings. One portion read "man is the most dangeroue anamal of all." The last third of the message stated, "I will not give you my name because you will try to sloi down or atop my collectiog of slaves."[35] Despite his earlier promise, the killer did not reveal his identity anywhere in the passage, unless he somehow hid it in a string of nineteen scrambled letters at the end of the third cipher message, but Innes says that "cipher experts concluded this was common practice [in cryptography], to fill out a message to the desired length."[36]

For years after the three-part enciphered letter was solved, the unidentified murderer, who began referring to himself as the Zodiac Killer in his correspondence, continued to kill people and to mail cards and letters to newspaper editors and police. No more of his letters were written in cipher, but Robert Graysmith, a former reporter for the *San Francisco Chronicle* and a longtime Zodiac researcher, says cryptologists "searched for hidden ciphers and messages" in all of the Zodiac's correspondence anyway, looking for clues. "Initial letters of words, first, second, third, last letters of words; line beginnings, line endings...did not spell anything,"[37] Graysmith says. The police

Researcher Robert Graysmith looks at a cryptograph sent by the Zodiac Killer.

were stymied. Then, for four years, from 1974 to 1978, the Zodiac Killer sent no correspondence at all. He eventually mailed what police believed to be the final genuine Zodiac letter in April 1978, which ended with the sentence, "I am now in control of all things."[38] No more Zodiac murders occurred after that.

The case of the Zodiac Killer is as notorious for its cipher puzzles as for its brutal murders. The Zodiac's penchant for cryptology has made this case one of the most studied and most memorable in U.S. crime history. "Nearly four decades after the initial crimes, it's become a regular obsession for some people to try to figure out the Zodiac's identity," says forensic psychologist and author Katherine Ramsland. "A few have even shouldered the challenge of revisiting the mathematical calculations, noting the errors made in earlier attempts [at cryptanalysis], but so far, these efforts have proven nothing conclusive."[39] More than 2,500 suspects in the case have been investigated over the years, but the case of the Zodiac Killer, who was responsible for at least seven slayings and who claimed in his letters that he had committed many more, remains unsolved. The identity of this criminal cryptographer may never be known.

Explosive Evidence Enciphered

On April 3, 1996, FBI investigators invaded a rural Montana cabin belonging to Theodore Kaczynski, the lead suspect in a criminal investigation of thirteen bombs that had been sent through the U.S. postal system over the course of nearly two decades. The bombs had killed three people and injured twenty-two others. The perpetrator was nicknamed the Unabomber because he targeted university and airline workers with his deadly packages. For eighteen years he had evaded detection.

Investigators finally tracked Kaczynski down based on a tip from his brother. They collected more than seven hundred pieces of evidence from his tiny cabin, including bomb parts. Perhaps the most telling evidence of all was the encrypted journals in which Kaczynski, a former math professor, described his crimes. He had used a complex cipher to disguise his writings, but because he had stored the key with the journals, federal agents quickly decrypted them. Kaczynski's case never went to trial; he pleaded guilty and was sentenced to life in prison in May 1998. His decrypted

Theodore Kaczynski's coded journals provided law enforcement with all the evidence they needed to convict him of his crimes.

journals, however, described his crimes in so much detail that they alone may have contained enough incriminating information to convict him.

Confessions in Code

The Zodiac Killer was successful at hiding behind his ciphers, but cryptology has contributed to the downfall of other killers. Murderers often chronicle their crimes in diaries or letters, though rarely as publicly as the Zodiac Killer did when he sent his cipher letters to newspapers to brag about what he had done. Some killers write down the stories of their crimes in a seeming attempt to unburden a guilty conscience. Such may have been the case for Joe Smith, a thirty-seven-year-old cocaine addict who abducted, raped, and murdered an eleven-year-old girl named Carlie Brucia in Sarasota, Florida, on February 1, 1994. The abduction, which happened on Superbowl Sunday, was captured on film by a security camera on the back of a car wash building Carlie had passed on her way home from a friend's house. The videotape of the kidnapping was later aired on the news, and calls poured in with tips. At least three callers identified the man on the tape as Smith.

Smith was on parole after serving time in prison for drug use. When police followed tips from callers and found him at his home, they also discovered drug paraphernalia, which was evidence that he had violated the terms of his parole. This gave police cause to arrest him immediately. When Carlie's body was discovered four days after the abduction, Smith was then also charged with her murder. The police had DNA evidence in the case—Smith allegedly left body fluids on Carlie's shirt—but perhaps even more incriminating than the DNA was a letter Smith wrote to his brother in a cipher system the two men had used when they were kids. The FBI's Cryptanalysis and Racketeering Unit (CCRU), which specializes in analyzing criminal communications written in ciphers or codes, deciphered the message. Smith had replaced letters of the alphabet with numbers and symbols in one- or two-character combinations. To make the letter even harder to read, he enciphered it backwards, starting at the bottom right corner of the page and ending at the top left. "Despite these obstacles, CRRU examiners were able to quickly decipher the message, which contained incriminating references to hiding evidence and moving the body," says the FBI's Web site. "A CRRU examiner presented the decryption evidence at Smith's trial."[40] Smith was convicted of Carlie Brucia's murder in November 2005 and was sentenced to death.

According to the FBI, evidence in many criminal cases involves the use of codes and cipher communication that the perpetrators believe will deter investigators. Cryptanalysts at the CRRU regularly analyze messages written by cryptographers who commit a wide variety of crimes—murders, gang violence, drug trafficking, white-collar crimes, gambling, computer hacking, and even domestic terrorist activities. Whatever type of criminal uses cryptology, there are always two sides to it: the need to disguise messages cleverly, and the need for the analysts who intercept those messages to be even more clever at solving them. Forensic cryptologists are basically tasked with solving puzzles, but they are puzzles with very high stakes indeed.

CHAPTER 3

Cracking Criminal Codes

In May 1993 the FBI opened an investigation into the activities of a man named Aldrich Ames, who had served in the U.S. Central Intelligence Agency (CIA) for thirty-one years. The FBI suspected that Ames had also been working as a Russian spy. They believed he had revealed the classified names of Russian agents working with the CIA and the FBI to the Russian government in exchange for payments totaling almost two million dollars. During the ten-month investigation, the FBI seized Ames' computers and found electronic documents that had been encrypted. "The investigator handling the computer evidence was able to break the codes,"[41] say Dorothy Denning, a computer science professor, and William E. Baugh Jr., former assistant director of the FBI. The decrypted documents linked Ames to the Russian foreign intelligence service and helped the FBI prove their case against him in court. Ames was found guilty of espionage and was sentenced to prison. "According to investigators," say Denning and Baugh, "failure to recover the encrypted data would have weakened the case."[42]

Ames' capture and conviction is a high-profile example of how criminals use cryptology to mask their secret communications, baffle investigators, and hide the evidence of their crimes. Encrypted messages "can be extremely valuable" to forensic investigations, say Denning and Baugh, because "they capture the subjects' own words, which generally holds up much better in court than information acquired from informants, for example, who are often criminals themselves and extremely unreliable."[43] Encrypted messages, when investigators can reveal them, are very incriminating forms of evidence. "In many criminal cases, documents and other papers found at a subject's premises provide evidence crucial for successful prosecution,"[44] say Denning and Baugh.

Forensic cryptanalysts are responsible for analyzing any encoded or enciphered messages criminals have used to plan or commit crimes. Cryptanalysis is not needed in every

Becoming a Forensic Cryptanalyst

Job Description:
Forensic cryptanalysts decrypt codes and cipher systems during investigations of criminal or national security threats. The FBI, the National Security Agency (NSA), and other federal and state law enforcement agencies are the main employers of cryptanalysts.

Education:
A bachelor's degree is required, usually in mathematics, computer science, or linguistics, but educational backgrounds of cryptanalysts vary. All candidates complete an intensive training program, such as the NSA's Cryptanalyst Development Program, to learn the skills they need for this job.

Qualifications:
Successful completion of a cryptanalysis training program is necessary, and candidates must meet all requirements to become an FBI or NSA agent if they are applying at one of those agencies. Mastery of at least one foreign language may also be a requirement.

Additional Information:
Patience, persistence, confidentiality, and a knack for creative problem solving are essential skills for this career. The job often involves long hours of tedious work. Foreign and domestic travel is sometimes required.

Salary:
$40,000 to more than $75,000 per year

investigation, but in some criminal cases, it is essential. "If nothing were decrypted," say Denning and Baugh, "many criminals would go free."[45] Cryptanalysts and their code-breaking skills can help investigators read criminal communications about crimes that are about to take place. They can also help prove a person's guilt in crimes that have already been committed, as they did in Ames' espionage case. Cryptanalysts have highly specialized skills that fill a small but important niche in the investigation of crime. As communication technology rapidly expands, their skills are becoming ever more important to forensic science.

Who Cryptanalysts Are

Those who are drawn to the field of forensic cryptanalysis come from a variety of backgrounds, skills, and interests. Often, they find their way into cryptanalysis from career paths that have nothing to do with crime investigation. Many cryptanalysts have been trained in mathematics or science, for example. Others have studied languages, music, or art. Don Harden, who solved the Zodiac Killer's newspaper ciphers, was a high school history and economics teacher. During World War II, when Great Britain's government was searching for code-breakers to add to its secret cryptanalysis team, it ran a newspaper puzzle contest to look for potential candidates among the general public. "Codebreakers can come from all areas," says cryptologist Daniel Olson, "and the best ones are often the ones you'd least expect."[46]

Despite having widely varied skills and interests, certain areas of expertise are common to people who become successful cryptanalysts. "Code breaking is absolutely a math function," says Olson. "You're solving X, like algebra. But math alone can't help you enter the mind of a criminal and figure out what they are communicating."[47] Math, therefore, is only one of the skills needed by a forensic cryptanalyst. Equally important is a strong knowledge of language and linguistics, because the process of breaking encrypted communication begins with looking for linguistic patterns among the letters, words, numbers, or symbols of

Cryptanalysts come from a variety of backgrounds and possess several skills and interests that help them decipher coded messages.

a message. Certain personality traits, too, are important. Patience, persistence, and intuition are essential to the science of breaking codes and ciphers without knowing the key. "This kind of work, particularly in the early stages of cryptanalysis, is perhaps the most excruciating, exasperating, agonizing mental process known to man," cryptology expert David Kahn says. "Hour after hour, day after day, sometimes month after month, the cryptanalyst tortures his brain to find some relationship between the letters"[48] of an encrypted message.

Cryptanalysts work behind the scenes, sometimes in secret rooms, usually with little more than brainpower and their knowledge of cryptology to assist them. Computers can be helpful for some of a cryptanalyst's most tedious tasks, but even in the computer age, computers have yet to match the puzzling power of the human mind. "I would be amazed to see a machine that can 'read' some of the codes and ciphers that have been used by criminals," says Olson. "The best machine available is a sharp mind and a sharp pencil."[49]

How Cryptanalysts Work

Forensic cryptanalysts have the job of analyzing a piece of writing—a plaintext—that has been disguised by some method to make it unreadable by unintended recipients. They are often presented with what appears to be a completely nonsensical jumble of letters, numbers, or symbols. Without having the key to crack the cipher, and often without even knowing the method criminals used to disguise the message in the first place, forensic cryptanalysts face a seemingly impossible task. They do not always succeed; some of the encrypted messages assigned to forensic cryptanalysts are never solved. Some messages, however, are solved in a matter of minutes, and the criminals' plans are quickly revealed. How cryptanalysts are able to transform seemingly nonsensical garble back into the original message may seem like magic to those unfamiliar with the science of cryptology. "Certainly the great geniuses in this art, as in every other, possess a quality of intellect that defies definition and mystifies more average minds,"[50] says crime science author Laurence Dwight Smith. But forensic cryptanalysts do have important clues at their disposal, as well as a specific plan of attack that usually enables them to see through the clusters of symbols to the message beneath.

Finding Hidden Messages

Before cryptanalysis can begin, a secret message must be intercepted. Usually the cryptanalysts themselves are not the ones who come across the secret communications. Throughout history, intercepting codes and ciphers has usually been the work of spies or traitors, such as the servant who betrayed Mary, Queen of Scots, and handed her notes over to her enemies. In modern times, police may have undercover agents

Cryptanalysts decoded thousands of encrypted messages sent by German and Japanese militaries during World War II.

who come across encoded messages from criminals, then either confiscate the notes or copy them before passing them on to their intended recipients. Sometimes, the messages that need to be analyzed are intercepted electronically, as in the thousands of messages sent over radio airwaves in World War II or criminal communications that are now transmitted by e-mail or text messaging. The easiest messages to intercept usually pose the greatest challenge for cryptanalysts, because if the authors of the encrypted messages do not even try to hide the existence of their communication, it usually means they have developed a complicated encryption system that they think will be extremely difficult or even impossible to crack. The German and Japanese militaries during World War II, for example, were very confident in their encryption methods when they sent radio messages. They knew the

Electing Security over Convenience

The United States is one of the world's most technologically advanced democracies—nations in which citizens vote for their leaders—but voter turnout for American elections is surprisingly low. In the 2008 presidential election, only about 57 percent of Americans old enough to vote actually did. Increasing voter turnout has been a goal of political activists for decades, and one way to do so could be letting people vote online instead of standing in line at a polling location.

Online voting could put the entire democratic process at the mercy of skilled computer hackers, however. The mere possibility that a devious interceptor could sneak into people's personal computers and change their votes, corrupt the votes collected, or even crash Internet hosts to prevent voters from getting online is an extremely serious concern, because it could destroy the nation's faith that its leaders were elected fairly. Cryptographers are always seeking new and better ways to encrypt digital information for security, and future generations of voters may see an era of cryptology in which votes can be securely cast online. But for now, cryptologists agree that the only way to protect elections from fraudsters, hoaxers, and political criminals is to have people vote the old way—in person.

Allied governments could intercept their communications easily, but they did not realize the Allies would also be able to understand them.

How and from whom an encrypted message was intercepted before it arrives on the desk of a forensic cryptanalyst gives important clues that can be used to begin solving the puzzle. The cryptanalyst asks about the general context of the message—who it came from, who was meant to receive it, and often, the topic of discussion. This background information gives valuable hints the cryptanalyst will use to begin attacking the message.

Knowing the Intended Audience

Cryptanalysts have a vested interest in knowing who wrote an encrypted message and who was supposed to receive it, because certain types of criminals—a particular prison gang, for example—may prefer certain methods of encryption for their messages such as substitution ciphers that replace each letter with a different letter or symbol. Forensic cryptanalysts who know this have a starting point and can approach the message as they would any substitution cipher.

When analyzing a cipher, cryptanalysts can often guess how difficult it will be to crack based on certain general details, such as if the message is handwritten or if it was computer-generated.

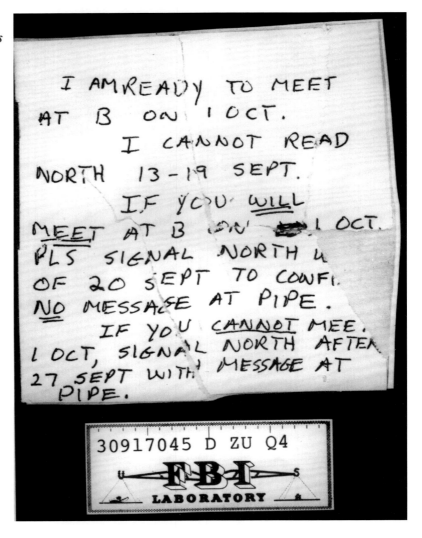

Even if the cryptanalyst is not told the identity of the sender and the recipient or even the particular gang or group the message came from, general details about the context of the message (whether it was handwritten on a restaurant napkin, for instance, or found in a computer file) will hint at how difficult the cryptanalysis will be. "The encryption and decryption method must not be too complicated" for the person who was meant to receive it,

By the Numbers

65%

Percentage of words in the English language that contain its most common letter, *e*

explains Bauer. "It must be appropriate to the intelligence and circumstances of the people who have to use it." Criminals who encipher messages realize that the task can be "easily overdone," says Bauer, "thereby making the message indecipherable to an intended recipient."[51] For this reason criminals generally choose the least complicated method of encryption the situation calls for. If an encrypted message was intercepted from a drug dealer on the street, for example, the cryptanalyst assumes that the method for encrypting the message must have been fairly simple for the intended recipient—possibly another drug dealer—to decode. If the message came from a technologically advanced group of Internet hackers, on the other hand, the forensic cryptanalyst can expect that an advanced method of encryption likely was used, possibly one that involved several different types of substitutions and the help of a computer. Such a message will be far more difficult to crack, and the cryptanalyst may use a different approach than that used for the message from the drug dealer.

A weakness of any encrypted criminal message, no matter how complex, is the use of common words and phrases. If forensic cryptanalysts know the context of an encrypted message, they can list words that the original message was likely to contain. Enciphered messages that have been intercepted from known drug dealers, for example, will likely contain nicknames, code names, or criminal slang words to stand in for the names of common drugs being sold and bought on city streets. Forensic

Cryptanalysts look for patterns in the way the symbols of a cipher behave, because this always reflects the way the letters in the original language behave.

cryptanalysts learn the common slang words in crime, such as the word *chalk*, a nickname for the drug methamphetamine. They may expect words like *chalk* to be hidden somewhere in the encrypted message of a drug dealer. A group of the same five letters or symbols that repeats multiple times in the message might be the word *chalk* in cipher form. If this turns out to be true, then the cryptanalyst has already solved five letters of the cipher and knows what symbols now stand for the letters *c, h, a, l,* and *k* throughout the message. "If you give a cryptanalyst an inch he takes a mile," says cryptographer and computer programmer Reinhard Wobst. Once a cryptanalyst has solved even a few letters of a cipher, "this is always the beginning of the end."[52]

Finding important slang words in a cipher message, however, depends on a third clue that comes from the context of the message: the language the original message was written in. Knowing the sender and the intended recipient of the message will often also reveal the language of the original message, and this is a cryptanalyst's most important hint. "All established languages have unique characteristics of grammar, syntax, sentence structure and spellings which can yield valuable clues,"[53] says Fred Wrixon, a military and espionage historian. Cryptanalysts looks for patterns in the way the symbols of a cipher behave, because this always reflects the way the letters in the original language behave. "Letters of language have 'personalities' of their own," says Kahn. "Though in a cryptogram they wear disguises, the cryptanalyst observes their actions and idiosyncrasies, and infers their identities from these traits."[54] When the cryptanalyst knows the situation for which the code or cipher was created, as well as the language the original plaintext message was written in, the tedious process of actually solving the message is already well under way.

The Case of the Long-lived Cipher

Edgar Allan Poe was an American author who lived in the 1800s. He is considered the inventor of the detective story and had a known fascination for cryptology. One of his short stories, "The Gold Bug," explained in detail how ciphers are solved. Poe also wrote essays on the subject. In 1840 the newspaper where he was an editor ran a contest for readers to submit a cipher Poe could not crack. More than a hundred entries flooded in. Poe easily solved all of them but two, which he said came from one W. B. Tyler. Poe published these ciphers in 1841, challenging his readers to send him the solutions. No one did. The ciphers remained unbroken until one was cracked by a literature professor in 1992. Two English professors and a math professor then created the Poe Cryptographic Challenge to see if anyone could solve Poe's second cipher. A Canadian software engineer provided the solution in October 2000. Some Poe scholars believe Poe created both ciphers himself under the fictitious name of W. B. Tyler. No doubt the famed author would have been pleased that it took 159 years for anyone to solve the mystery.

Decrypting a Message

The solution of any encrypted message, no matter how complicated it seems, begins with poring over the material, looking for ways that the new symbols or characters might behave like the original letters they are masking. Kahn calls this initial analysis the most universal and basic of cryptanalytic procedures. "No cryptogram [code or cipher] was ever solved by staring at it,"[55] he says. To uncover an encrypted message, the cryptanalyst uses a combination of linguistics (the study of the

Cryptanalysts use a variety of tools when deciphering codes, including the principles of language structure and mathematical probability.

	A B C D E F G H I J K L M N O P Q R S T U V W X Y Z
A	A B C D E F G H I J K L M N O P Q R S T U V W X Y Z
B	B C D E F G H I J K L M N O P Q R S T U V W X Y Z A
C	C D E F G H I J K L M N O P Q R S T U V W X Y Z A B
D	D E F G H I J K L M N O P Q R S T U V W X Y Z A B C
E	E F G H I J K L M N O P Q R S T U V W X Y Z A B C D
F	F G H I J K L M N O P Q R S T U V W X Y Z A B C D E
G	G H I J K L M N O P Q R S T U V W X Y Z A B C D E F
H	H I J K L M N O P Q R S T U V W X Y Z A B C D E F G
I	I J K L M N O P Q R S T U V W X Y Z A B C D E F G H
J	J K L M N O P Q R S T U V W X Y Z A B C D E F G H I
K	K L M N O P Q R S T U V W X Y Z A B C D E F G H I J
L	L M N O P Q R S T U V W X Y Z A B C D E F G H I J K
M	M N O P Q R S T U V W X Y Z A B C D E F G H I J K L
N	N O P Q R S T U V W X Y Z A B C D E F G H I J K L M
O	O P Q R S T U V W X Y Z A B C D E F G H I J K L M N
P	P Q R S T U V W X Y Z A B C D E F G H I J K L M N O
Q	Q R S T U V W X Y Z A B C D E F G H I J K L M N O P
R	R S T U V W X Y Z A B C D E F G H I J K L M N O P Q
S	S T U V W X Y Z A B C D E F G H I J K L M N O P Q R
T	T U V W X Y Z A B C D E F G H I J K L M N O P Q R S
U	U V W X Y Z A B C D E F G H I J K L M N O P Q R S T
V	V W X Y Z A B C D E F G H I J K L M N O P Q R S T U
W	W X Y Z A B C D E F G H I J K L M N O P Q R S T U V
X	X Y Z A B C D E F G H I J K L M N O P Q R S T U V W
Y	Y Z A B C D E F G H I J K L M N O P Q R S T U V W X
Z	Z A B C D E F G H I J K L M N O P Q R S T U V W X Y

cipher	VVVRBACP
key	COVERCOVER...
plaintext	THANKYOU

structure of language) and math concepts, especially statistics and probability. "An analyst generally begins an assault on a cryptomethod by counting the letters, numbers and any other symbols used and by noting with which other letters or figures they appear,"[56] says Wrixon. The cryptanalyst then makes a table of all the letters or symbols that appear in the message and tallies the number of times that each one occurs. This table is called a frequency chart, which Wrixon says is "a primary clue for a cryptanalyst, because every legitimate language has discernible patterns for vowels, consonants, and syllable pairs."[57] In other words, certain letters in any language can be expected to appear in messages more often than others. Therefore, using the frequency chart and knowing the most common letters in a language, the cryptanalyst can begin to make guesses about which symbols in the message may stand for which letters of the plaintext.

> ## By the Numbers
>
> ## 3
>
> **Number of mathematicians employed by the FBI in 2010**

For messages written in English, cryptanalysts use the made-up word ETAONRISH to remember the nine most common letters used in the English language. Accordingly, the symbol that appears most often in an encrypted message is likely to stand for the letter *e*, and the second most common letter might well be a *t* or an *a*. "Infrequently used letters such as *q*, *x* and *z* are also important, since they may be covered by enciphered letters that occur only a few times," says Wrixon. When letter frequency is analyzed, certain patterns in the message may begin to reveal themselves. "Codes and ciphers cannot be solved by simply comparing frequencies to standard lists of letter usage," Wrixon says. "Still, once letters have been found to show some frequency tendencies, these patterns are studied."[58]

When cryptanalysts have a pretty good idea which cipher symbol stands for a common letter, such as *e*, they may then look for patterns of two or more symbols containing the one that could be *e*. "Most languages have letters that typically operate in pairs and other letters that rarely meet," says Wrixon. "The characters or numerals that conceal them may therefore show some of the same tendencies."[59] In English, for example, the vowels *e* and *a* occur together in many words, such as *each*, *tear*, or *weapon*. The vowels *e* and *o*, in words like *people* or *amoeba*, occur together far less often. "Every letter has a cluster of preferred associations that constitute its most distinguishing characteristic,"[60] says Kahn. If cryptanalysts have a symbol they think is *e* and a second one that could be *o* or *a*, they are more likely to assume it is *a*, because that letter is more commonly paired with *e*. They will test this theory by replacing the two symbols with *e* and *a* throughout the message to see if this seems to give them parts of real words. "These trial-and-error tests are known as anagramming,"[61] says Wrixon. It is an important part of solving encrypted messages. It is also tedious, because if the cryptanalyst's guesses seem to be wrong—that is, anagramming does not result in logical words or parts of words in the encrypted message—he must try something different.

Consonants, even more often than vowels, tend to pair up more frequently with certain letters than with others. The combination of the consonants *th* and *sh*, for example, are common in the English language, whereas *n* and *h* very rarely occur together. In Spanish, the consonant *ñ* almost always occurs between two vowels, as in the word *mañana* (tomorrow) or *niño* (boy), but not at the beginning of words or next to other consonants. "Frequency lists are especially helpful when there is a pattern of repetitive letters," says Wrixon. For example, the repeated symbols *zz* or *$$* in an encrypted message may very well stand for *ee* or *ss* in English, or *rr* in Spanish. "Cryptanalysts must be careful of leaping to conclusions,"[62] Wrixon says, because some seemingly obvious letter pairs can give false leads, but often a cryptanalyst finds pairs of cipher symbols that logically stand in for letters of the original language, and a portion of the puzzle is solved. "The camouflage" of a cipher "does not alter the features of the underlying language,"[63] Kahn says.

In addition to common letters and letter pairs, cryptana-lysts look for repeating sequences of characters in the encrypted message that mask short but common words in the original language, such as *of*, *an*, *and*, or *the* in English. Just as the let-ters of every language appear with a certain frequency, so do the words of the language. The search for common words in a message may be combined with a search for words the forensic cryptanalyst thinks are likely to appear, such as names of the criminal's partners or associates, or slang words that the crimi-nal is likely to use. When a common word is found, the solution to the entire message usually is not far behind. "All it is now is a kind of guess, guided by the porous laws of probability,"[64] says Kahn. The cryptanalyst goes through the message, replacing symbols with plaintext letters and testing the results. Using these basic techniques, says Wrixon, "a cryptanalyst is well on the way to breaking a cipher's defenses." The final proof, he says, "is in the discovery of sensible words."[65]

Cryptology in Criminals' Hands

When forensic cryptanalysts are successful at revealing a crimi-nal message disguised by ciphers and codes, investigators often use that message as evidence to charge someone with a crime. Decrypted messages may also help police to know where cer-tain crimes, such as major drug deals or even terrorist attacks, are going to happen next. But cryptanalysts are not always successful at solving codes and ciphers to reveal the messages underneath. Much of today's crime involves computers, the Internet, and the theft of people's personal information. With advances in computer technology, many criminal encryption methods have also become increasingly complex. Certain kinds of ciphers are easy for an experienced cryptanalyst to solve, but some encrypted messages have undergone several levels of changes for added security; the plaintext message may be encrypted by one method, then the result may be encrypted by again by a different method. Solving such complex messages may be very time-consuming, or even impossible. "I would like to say that I spend every day breaking codes, but it seems that

I do more 'code looking at' than code breaking,"[66] says Olson. He says some codes are broken in minutes, but he also recalls one that took the FBI twenty years to break.

Advancements in computer technology are troubling to cryptanalysts for another reason. Not only do they make many criminal codes more difficult to solve, but criminals themselves are getting better at cryptanalysis, trying to break the very codes that law-abiding citizens now use to protect their own personal and financial information. In some ways criminals have turned the tables on forensic cryptologists; codes are not just cracked by police agencies trying to solve crimes anymore, they are also cracked by lawbreakers to *commit* crime. Public safety, in modern times, often depends on the ability of cryptologists to protect the private information of law-abiding people from criminals seeking to break codes.

CHAPTER 4

Hiding Data from Criminals

In the 1970s a period known as the information age began in the United States and quickly spread around the world. Marked by a massive increase in the amount of personal data kept and shared by computers, the information age changed the way people store, send, and find information. It also affected the science of cryptology. As digital files have replaced paper records not just in people's homes but in hospitals, banks, and corporations, it has become possible for criminals with a background in computer programming and technology to gain access to private information by breaking into computer systems. Computer programmers faced the challenge of finding secure ways to mask secret information stored in computers to protect it from being stolen or intercepted by criminal cryptanalysts trying to access data they are not meant to know.

The information age marked the birth of a new branch of crime, called "cybercrime," or illegal activity committed using computers and the Internet. Cybercrime, say Jack M. Balkin and Nimrod Kozlovski of the Information Society Project at Yale Law School, "requires us to redesign digital architectures to reduce the risk of criminal conduct and security breaches in the first place."[67] Cryptology is the solution to the increasing problem of protecting private information from the prying eyes of criminals.

The Birth of Digital Security

The need for codes to protect the private information of every citizen became obvious in the last quarter of the twentieth century. Computers had become commonplace in homes and businesses, and the Internet, a data-sharing network that connects computers all around the world, was developed along with other advances in computer technology. In 1969, researchers at the University of California, Los Angeles, and the Stanford Research Institute three hundred miles to the north made the first long-distance contact between computers. In 1971 a computer engineer named Ray Tomlinson typed and sent the first e-mail through a program he created to send simple messages to any computer connected to a network called ARPAnet (an ancestor of the modern Internet). That same year the first computer virus infected the ARPAnet, taking the form of a mischievous e-mail message: "Catch me if you can."[68]

Although that first virus and its anonymous writer did no real damage, they were a sign of a great threat. They proved that an unknown person with the right technology skills could infiltrate

Public Encryption Enemy Number One

In 1990 a Los Angeles radio station gave a Porsche to the 102nd caller in a promotional contest. The winner, Kevin Poulsen, had scrambled the station's twenty-five phone lines to make sure he was number 102. Poulsen was already on the run from the FBI at the time for repeatedly hacking into federal law enforcement and Defense Department databases. He evaded capture for seventeen months while continuing his computer crime streak with episodes like his radio station fraud. In 1991 he was featured on the television program *Unsolved Mysteries*, but he used a computer to disable the TV station's toll-free phone line so that no one could call in with tips as to his whereabouts. Poulsen was later captured in a grocery store. It took the FBI months to decrypt ten thousand pages of evidence Poulsen had hidden on his computer under several layers of complex encryption. He served fifty-one months in jail, one of the most severe sentences ever given for computer hacking. Poulsen is said to live an honest life now, but he is one of history's most notorious criminal masters of cryptology.

a computer system, possibly change computer programs, cause the system to stop working properly, steal and read private information, and even send e-mail messages while pretending to be someone else. Computer users needed to protect their computers and their private information from such dangers. "The information society [needed] to have a totally new security awareness," says programmer Reinhard Wobst. Because so much information is now stored in computers, he says, the risks of data theft and manipulation in the computer world "are different and sometimes even greater than in the physical world."[69]

The answer to the problem of data security was encryption, or masking digital data with a cipher system so complex it would be unbreakable for criminals. The ability of computers both to make codes and break them took the science of cryptology to a new level. Traditionally, cryptanalysts have solved codes and ciphers created by people, thereby pitting one person's cleverness against another to find the solution. Logic and practice are still a cryptanalyst's best tools for solving human-designed codes and ciphers, so forensic cryptanalysts who decrypt the handmade communications of murderers, drug dealers, and other crooks are not obsolete. But computers can generate complex codes and ciphers much more quickly than people can, and they can also solve complex codes by the brute force method, rapidly testing all possible solutions to an encrypted message until they find one that works. Thus, cryptology has evolved to include the making and breaking of *computer-made* codes and ciphers. Encryption methods must now be crafted to keep a step ahead of the cybercriminals who use computers as cryptanalytic tools and persistently try to break the codes that keep personal information safe. Digital security for computers has brought about the most complex encryption methods known to society.

Masking Data with Codes

To protect computer users from criminals trying to spy on them or steal their data, the U.S. government approved a digital security method in 1976 that it deemed a secure system for any

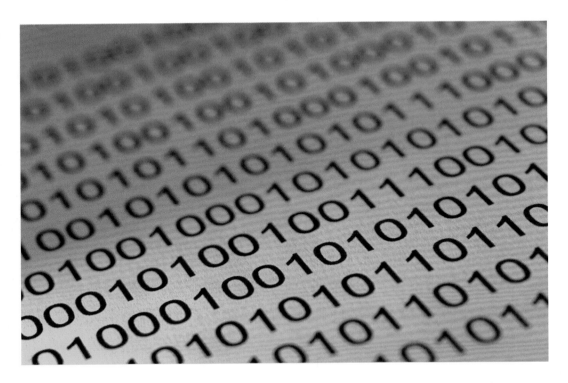

Binary code, written in zeroes and ones, is used to disguise data and encrypt plaintext.

computer. Called Data Encryption Standard (DES), it used a cipher method for disguising data such as the contents of a text file. Using DES, a computer chose one of a huge number of encryption methods, or algorithms, to replace the individual characters of a plaintext message with different ones. The finished product appeared as nonsense to any person or computer that did not have the algorithm, or key, for reversing the process. With any cipher method, the more complicated the key used to create it, the harder the encrypted message will be to decipher. DES keys were 56 bits long. Bits, or binary digits, are the smallest units of computer data. In computer programming each bit can be either a 1 or a 0, so a 56-bit key, with each bit having one of two possible values, created about 72 quadrillion possible DES keys for a computer to use to encrypt its data. Any unauthorized computer that intercepted a DES-encrypted message would have to test these 72 quadrillion possible keys, one by one, to find the key that could decrypt the message's information. No computers were powerful enough in the 1970s to do that task efficiently, so a DES-encrypted message was generally considered safe.

Computers evolved rapidly, however. Faster computer hardware and larger memory capacity made some computers powerful enough to test all possible solutions for a 56-bit key to find the right one. In 1999 distributed.net, a nonprofit organization of computer hobbyists, cracked a DES-encrypted message in only twenty-two hours as part of a contest to see whether a DES code could be solved, and, if so, how quickly. "The [Data Encryption Standard] and 56-bit cryptography are dead,"[70] said David McNett, cofounder of distributed.net, after his organization proved that the outdated 56-bit key could be solved in less than one day. Digital information encrypted with DES was no longer secure.

In the year 2000, a far more secure encryption system called Advanced Encryption Standard (AES) replaced DES as the method the government recommended for protecting private data. Whereas DES used a 56-bit key system with 72 quadrillion possible keys, AES has different versions, each with increasing security: a 128-bit, a 192-bit, or a 256-bit key system. In the 128-bit key system, the least secure of the three versions, the key is so long that a computer would have to test out 3×10^{38} (that is, a three with thirty-eight zeroes following it) different combinations to find the right one. In the 256-bit key system, the most secure of the three AES versions, there are 1×10^{77} (a one with seventy-seven zeroes following it) possible keys. According to the National Institute of Standards and Technology (NIST), if there were a computer that could crack a 56-bit key in just *one* second, "it would take that machine approximately 149 thousand-billion [149 trillion] years to crack a 128-bit AES key. To put that into perspective, the universe

> **By the Numbers**
>
> # 1 TRILLION
>
> **Approximate number of years it would take to crack the strongest known encryption key if a billion computers were working together, each processing a billion calculations per second**

is believed to be less than 20 billion years old."[71] No computers yet exist that are powerful enough to crack even a 128-bit key, much less a 256-bit key. The search for one key in such a huge range of possibilities "would be like trying to find one particular grain of sand in the Sahara desert,"[72] says computer systems engineer Jeff Tyson. Information that is encrypted with an AES system, for now, is considered extremely safe.

Dodging Encryption Methods

Despite the high level of security provided by AES encryption, cybercriminals do manage to break into computer systems to read or steal important data. Not all information in a computer is necessarily encrypted, especially if it is never sent over the Internet to another computer. Encrypted files are large and take up a lot of computer memory, so information just sitting in a hard drive and never shared online is rarely encrypted with AES. Anyone who is able to access a computer's hard drive, therefore, may be able to read or copy unencrypted files.

Password-protected computers and networks work as the first line of defense against cybercriminals.

Because multiple computers in a company or organization may also share the same local-area network (LAN), which connects all the computers in the organization so they can share files across the network, a cybercriminal who breaks into a single computer in a LAN could access other non-encrypted information in the organization.

Most computers and networks are password-protected to prevent such breaches of security. This fact poses the first obstacle to a cybercriminal, but it is a barrier that a determined hacker can often get around. "The best way to get into a system is to 'trick' the system into thinking you're an authorized user," says Internet technology expert Debra Littlejohn Shinder. "The vast majority of networks rely solely on [passwords], so anyone who knows or can guess the correct password with a valid username can get in."[73] A computer password is a vital tool for criminals, because it can be used not only to access a computer or a network, but often, to log onto e-mail servers and secure Web sites or to open password-protected documents as well. When cybercriminals do not know a password, they often use cryptanalysis to discover it. This is called "password cracking."

The process of cracking a password often involves the brute-force method—simply trying out every possible combination of letters, numbers, and symbols that the password could be. "Brute force might not be the most elegant solution for a hacker in search of a password," says Shinder, "but it can be very effective."[74] Sometimes, cybercriminals undertake the brute-force method by hand using standard techniques of cryptanalysis, but often, they use password-cracking computer software that tries all possible combinations in search of the password that works. "Some of these programs are very sophisticated and allow the cracker to implement rules or criteria"[75] in the search, says Shinder. For example, if the hacker knows how

By the Numbers

14

Minimum number of characters needed for a computer password to be reasonably safe from password cracking software

A computer password is a vital tool for a cybercriminal. Leaving a password where someone can find it could give them easy access to e-mail, secure Web sites, or profitable data.

many characters the password has and that it is alphanumeric (it contains both letters and numbers), this information can help the program narrow down the possible list of passwords. Thus, it will take less time to find one that works. Password-cracking software programs are readily available to users who need them for honest reasons, such as losing or forgetting an important password. "But of course," says Shinder, "the same software can be used for less-than-legitimate purposes."[76] Password-cracking software provides an easy way for cybercriminals to break into a computer system.

Not all computers have user passwords that are simple to crack, especially in industries such as national defense or multimillion dollar businesses, where keeping information secret is critically important. Such organizations typically have different levels of security for different users. Lower-level employees may have easy passwords to solve, but these employees' access to information may also be extremely limited. Other computers in the network might require much more complex passwords that are quite difficult to crack. If a hacker is able to cryptanalyze the password of even one computer in the network, however, it may be possible to obtain access to other passwords, particularly if a list of passwords exists somewhere in one of the network's computers. "In some cases," says Internet specialist Michael Cross, "that's exactly what happens—the list is right there for the taking on the computer's hard disk."[77] Passwords have to be stored somewhere, Cross explains. "After all, how else would your system know whether a user has entered the correct password?"[78]

Even if a hacker comes across a list of passwords on a hard drive, though, there usually is still one level of security protecting them. "In most cases, passwords are not stored in a plaintext file that the cracker can simply open and read," Cross says. "Usually, stored passwords are encrypted."[79] The hacker then

Hints Dropped by Hackers

When an intruder breaches a computer's security, he usually leaves warning signs. The following are some of the most common:

- Free space on the computer's hard drive suddenly vanishes and/or the computer runs extremely slowly, a sign that an intruder may be using the computer from a remote location.
- Programs or files disappear from the computer.
- People receive e-mails or attachments that appear to come from the computer owner but that he or she never sent.
- The computer's antivirus software suddenly crashes.
- The cursor starts moving around by itself or new Internet browser windows open on their own.

These signs should not be ignored. Hackers use victims' computers in all sorts of illegal ways. Theft of information is one danger, but a hacked computer can also be a storage place for illegal content such as pornography, making innocent victims appear guilty of crimes. If anyone suspects a computer is being hacked, he or she should report it to the FBI's Internet Crime Complaint Center.

must use cryptanalysis again to try to determine the encryption method, generate all the possible password combinations, encrypt each possible password with the proper method, and try each result in the network to see if one of them works. "Trying to guess passwords, even with software to expedite the process, is a tedious business,"[80] Cross says. But when the information the cybercriminal wants is very important, the monotonous work is worthwhile, because it could lead to data that will be very profitable to dishonest users.

How Criminals Use Information

Once a cybercriminal has skirted a computer system's passwords or other security measures and has gained access to private information, a wide range of crimes is possible. One option is extortion, or threatening to do something bad to someone unless a payoff is made. For example, if a cybercriminal breaks into a computer system and gains access to valuable trade secrets, such as a major food manufacturer's secret recipes, the criminal can then threaten to expose this information to the company's competitors unless the company pays money. "Information represents an asset," says Wobst, and "often embodies a much greater value than material things."[81] Companies may be tempted to give in to an extortionist's demands, because the leaking of private information may cost the company a fortune. Unfortunately, simply paying off an extortionist will not solve the company's problems. The extortionist, after all, has breached the organization's secrets and still possesses its information. Also, says attorney Beryl A. Howell, "the scope of the breach is usually far more serious than the initial problem suggests."[82] To restore the victim's security, the extortionist must be caught.

Howell describes one case of extortion that involved secret company information stolen during a computer system breach. The criminal, a disgruntled former customer, was able to get around the company's e-mail security methods and threatened to send a negative e-mail to all of the company's clients with the company's name in the message header. This could have resulted in a huge loss of business for the company. The criminal demanded a payoff of several million dollars to refrain from sending the e-mails. Fortunately, he was caught before he could carry out his extortion scheme. The story had a happy ending," says Howell, "at least from the perspective of the targeted company,"[83] but it took a concerted law-enforcement effort to track down the extortionist.

Another popular type of cybercrime committed by getting around encrypted information is fraud, a deliberate deception for personal gain. One of the most common types of cybercrime is credit card fraud, in which criminals obtain other people's credit card numbers and identifying information in order to use their accounts. Consumers often share their credit card account information with online vendors to buy things, which gives cybercriminals many opportunities to get their hands on credit card information. Any reputable vendor, of course, has a secure Web site that encrypts all credit card information with a highly secure method; even if a criminal intercepts account numbers on their way from the buyer's computer to the vendor's, the numbers are protected with public-key encryption, a two-part cipher that is all but impossible to crack. However, customers' unencrypted credit card

Although buyers' credit card numbers are protected by a two-part cipher that is all but impossible to crack, a cybercriminal could access the account numbers by breaking into the vendor's computer where the unencrypted information in stored.

Becoming a Cybercrime Investigator

Job Description:
In crimes that involve a computer or network intrusion, a cybercrime investigator recovers computer evidence that can be used by police to make an arrest, and later, by prosecutors in court. Most cybercrime investigators are employed by law enforcement agencies, software development companies, or firms with large computer networks.

Education:
Cybercrime investigators need a bachelor's degree in computer science with additional coursework in criminal science, computer forensics, and cybercrime studies.

Qualifications:
Cybercrime investigators can achieve certification by completing the Certified Forensic Computer Examiner (CFCE) Program of the International Association of Computer Investigative Specialists. Many employers require cybercrime investigators to be certified.

Additional Information:
Computer crime is among the fastest-growing types of crime in the world, so job opportunities for cybercrime investigators are numerous. Some investigators work as freelance consultants. Cybercrime investigators must actively continue their education, because the field advances rapidly.

Salary:
$50,000 to more than $100,000 a year

information is often stored in the vendor's computer records after a purchase. Therefore, if a cybercriminal can break into the *vendor's* computer system, he may be able to access account numbers that he can then use illegally.

In 2009 Albert Gonzalez, a computer hacker in Miami,

Florida, was arrested for doing just that. He was charged with the theft of more than 130 million credit and debit card numbers he had obtained from hacking into the sites of several major chain stores, including Target and 7-11, and of a credit-card processing company in New Jersey. It was the largest theft of credit and debit card data ever to occur in the United States. Gonzalez found ways around his victims' computer-security systems to steal the data. He pleaded guilty to the crime and will serve between seventeen and twenty-five years in prison, but his case demonstrates the ever-present threat of cybercriminals and the need to track them down as soon as possible once they breach the security of a computer system. This is the job of cybercrime investigators.

Solving Cybercrime with Cryptology

The investigation of cybercrime is similar to any other type of forensic investigation. "The crimes that are being committed haven't changed, just the manner in which they're being committed,"[84] say Anthony Reyes and Jack Wiles, experts on computer security and cybercrime investigation. As in any criminal investigation, therefore, cybercrime investigators must try to discover what crime occurred, how it was committed, and who was responsible. The major difference is that in the computer world, most crimes are committed at a distance from the crime scene—sometimes from across the country or even across the world—and the only connection between the criminal and victim is usually through a computer network. "With cyber crimes, there is no collateral or forensic evidence, such as eyewitnesses, fingerprints, or DNA," say Reyes and Wiles. Sometimes, they say, cyber criminals even seem to lack a motive; they commit their crimes for the thrill of it or because they want to "leave a mark."[85] Most crimes committed through computers are not personal crimes motivated by revenge or anger. They are crimes of opportunity. Cybercriminals are always trying to exploit systems that have weaknesses in security.

Often, cybercrimes are also anonymous. Hackers can spy

on private information from a distance without ever disclosing their identities, and it may be a long time before the victims even realize their systems have been invaded. Investigators therefore have a difficult challenge, because the perpetrator is most likely a complete stranger to the cybercrime victims. The only lead that cybercrime investigators have is a trail of digital evidence, however well hidden, that will lead them to the hacker. Often, investigators use principles of cryptology to help them track down computer hackers. The Internet, after all, is a world of codes that connects computers together and distinguishes one computer from another. This makes computers traceable and can lead investigators to important evidence in a crime.

Every computer is encoded with a unique Internet Protocol address (or "identity"), which makes it very difficult to commit cybercrimes anonymously.

One important clue in a cybercrime investigation is a computer-specific code, called an Internet Protocol (IP) address, which every computer needs to access the Internet. "Every computer connected to the Internet … has a unique Internet Protocol (IP) address,"[86] says computer technology reporter

Andrew Kantor. The IP is a group of numbers that encodes the identity of a computer, and every computer's IP is different. "It's used to identify you so when you visit a Web site, that site knows how to send those pages to you," Kantor says. "Think of it as the equivalent of a stamped, self-addressed envelope: If you want any information to come to you—whether it's e-mail, a Web page, or what have you—you need to tell the rest of the world where you are."[87] Any computer's Internet connection and its corresponding IP code create evidence that can be traced. "The very acts of connecting your computer to the Net, browsing sites, sending mail…they all leave traces behind,"[88] says Kantor.

When investigating a cybercrime, police can contact the Internet provider a suspect used to log on to the Internet. The provider will have a record of the computer (and computer owner) connected to the IP address in question. Experienced cybercriminals know this, so they may find ways to break the link between their online criminal activity and their IP address. They may use a university computer lab instead of their home computer, for example, or they may log onto the Internet only through anonymous browsers that hide IP addresses from Web servers. "Even then, though," says Kantor, "at some point the information has to get to their desktops. It's hard to be completely anonymous."[89] IP addresses, therefore, are important cryptologic evidence in a cybercrime. These computer-identifying codes often lead investigators to the exact location (the computer) where the criminal activity took place.

Another cryptology tool valuable for cybercrime investigations is a digital signature, an encrypted tag that can be attached to the documents or messages a particular user creates, much like a handwritten signature on a paper document. A digital signature proves that one particular computer user, and no other, created a document. In a forensic investigation of a computer crime, the existence of a digital signature proves the real author of a document. Digital signatures can be used as evidence of criminal activity; a person who denies typing a malicious document or sending a crime-related e-mail is proven guilty if her encrypted digital signature is attached to the evidence. Digital signatures can also be used to prove the innocence of someone accused of creating a criminal document or e-mail, if its digital signature belongs to someone else. Unlike a handwritten signature, an encoded digital signature is impossible to forge or counterfeit.

Investigators also use a form of encryption called a message digest as evidence in cybercrime cases. A message digest is a version of a document that is condensed, encrypted, and then attached to the original document. It is basically an encrypted summary of the document's exact contents. Once a message digest for a document has been created, it can never be changed, even if the original document is altered. Thus, if a document is intercepted by a third party and modified at all, the message digest will not exactly match the original document. It will show that the document has been changed after it left the possession of the original author. This can be used as evidence in cases where criminals have falsified documents or pretended to be someone else online and in e-mail.

A Tangled Web of Codes

Cryptology tools like digital signatures and message digests help prevent people from becoming victims of computer crime and make it easier for investigators to recognize and trace criminal activity. However, these measures are not guaranteed to be foolproof forever. Cryptographers who encrypt private information always tend to be matched at each step by crypanalysts who devise ways to get around their safeguards. "Criminals often afford the newest toys and desire the most complex technologies to hide their crimes from prying eyes," say Reyes and Wiles. "The data forensics community must always strive to master technologies as fast as technology evolves."[90] Future advances in computer technology will make cryptology even more complex, and the task of catching criminals who use it will only get more challenging.

CHAPTER 5

The Future of Cryptology

S taying a step ahead of criminals who use cryptology either to mask their own communication or to steal other people's private information has wide-reaching effects on society. If cryptologists do not detect and put a stop to criminal activity, they may fail in their efforts to keep citizens safe. Wherever there are cryptographers inventing encryption methods, there are also cryptanalysts trying to find a way around those methods. This tug of war between creating secure encryption methods and breaking them has spread across the information society, which now spans the globe. Anywhere there are computers and Internet connections, concerns exist about information's security, about people's privacy, and about how much leeway governments should have to manage the encryption and decryption of information. These are issues that will challenge the field of forensic cryptology in the years to come.

Quantum Cryptography

Advancement in computer technology knows no bounds, and the field of cryptology must therefore advance too. Today's Advanced Encryption Standard (AES) creates ciphers that make it a virtual impossibility for any computer that exists in the modern world to crack an encrypted message. AES methods are the most advanced cryptology tools available—but in the future, they may no longer be strong enough to keep out eavesdroppers. "Current computers will be replaced in the near future with quantum computers," says journalist Josh Clark. "These computers are expected to be able to perform calculations and operate at speeds no computer in use now could possibly achieve."[91] Scientists believe quantum computers, which

Encrypting E-mails

When two computer users want to exchange secure e-mail over the Internet, they can use a Public Key Encryption program to disguise content so that only the recipient can read what the sender wrote. Public Key Encryption works like this:

1 The sender composes a message and clicks *send*.

2 The recipient receives a notice that the sender wants to communicate.

3 The recipient has two keys, a private key he never shares and a public key he sends to anyone who wants it. He gives his public key to the sender of the e-mail (similar to passing her a briefcase and its key).

4 The sender uses the recipient's public key to encrypt the message (like putting the message into his briefcase and locking it).

5 The sender passes the encrypted message (the briefcase) back to the recipient.

6 The recipient gets the encrypted message (the locked briefcase). The lock is special, because it takes *two* keys to open it again (to decrypt the message): the public key the recipient shares openly *and* his private key, which he never shares. Because only the recipient has both keys, only he can unlock (decrypt) the message that was sent to him.

could replace today's models by the year 2020 or sooner, will be able to work on a million calculations at once; today's average desktop computer can only manage one calculation at a time. Quantum computers could level the playing field of

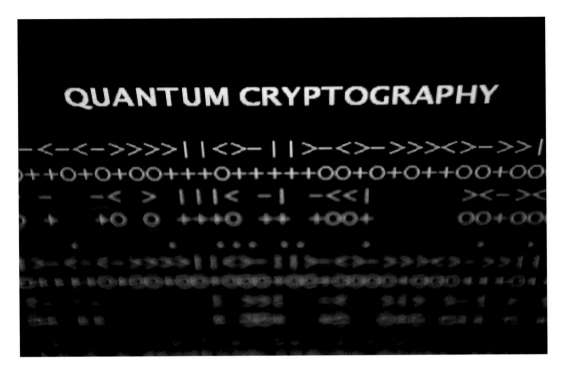

cryptology, providing the processing power to match what is required by today's encryption methods and solve AES ciphers within days.

Fortunately, newer, more secure systems for protecting information through cryptology are being developed too. The concept of quantum computers is based on physics—the study of matter, energy, and how the two are related—on an extremely tiny scale that involves photons, the smallest known particles of light. These particles will carry information within a quantum computer. In quantum cryptology, photons are also used to encrypt data and provide the key for decrypting it. Photons spin in all different directions unless they are passed through a filter that captures their spin and locks it into one particular direction. The following is a simplified explanation of how quantum cryptology works: Computer 1 passes a stream of spinning photos through its photon filter to lock the spin of each photon into one of four different directions—vertical, horizontal, diagonally to the left, or diagonally to the right. The photon stream is

In the future, quantum cryptography will completely safeguard private communications.

then sent to a recipient, Computer 2, which captures the photons in its own filter. When the photons hit Computer 2's filter, the computer can "read" the direction of each photon's spin, and thus, determine the code—the series of spin directions that will be used by Computer 1's photons to encrypt a private message to Computer 2. Computer 2 then checks back with Computer 1 to see if the code it received is correct. If it is, this code will be their key for encrypting and decrypting private information.

What will make quantum cryptology so effective at hiding messages is that the direction of a photon's spin changes any time it passes through a filter. A key, therefore, can only be sent to one recipient. That recipient's filter will read the directions of the photon's spins as they hit the filter, but then the directions of the spins will change as they pass through the filter, destroying the code. The same stream of photons cannot carry the same code to any other recipient. So if a code sent from Computer 1 to Computer 2 is intercepted along the way by an eavesdropper (Computer A), the directions of the photons' spins will be entirely different when Computer A passes them on to Computer 2. Computer 2 and Computer 1 will compare their versions of the code, and the versions will not match, so they will know that an eavesdropper intercepted the code with its own filter to listen in. They will not send messages back and forth using that code.

"In modern cryptology," says Clark, "an eavesdropper can passively intercept an encrypted message and work to decode it without the sender knowing. Quantum cryptology is the first cryptology that safeguards against passive interception."[92] This gives quantum cryptology a tremendous advantage over number-based AES methods, which can be easily intercepted by Computer A without the knowledge of Computers 1 and 2. Currently, a message's only defense against eavesdroppers is the strength of the key used to encrypt it. Quantum cryptology, however, will completely safeguard private communications.

Although quantum physics may one day be very useful for cryptology, it is a very confusing concept. Even physicists still have much to learn and understand about how quantum computers and encryption methods will work. In the world of forensic science, complexity is not always a good thing, because any methods or evidence used to prove guilt of a crime are eventually scrutinized in a court of law during the alleged criminal's trial. If courtroom evidence is as complicated as quantum physics, the judge and the jury members may find it so confusing that they cannot make sense of it. If they cannot understand the evidence, they also cannot use it to guide their decisions about whether to convict someone of

Security Up in the Air

Airplanes have long been popular targets for terrorists, as was tragically demonstrated when hijacked airplanes crashed into both towers of the World Trade Center on September 11, 2001. In the past, terrorists had to board planes to carry out their crimes, but with computer technology, they may now be able to stage their attacks from remote locations. Cyber attacks on the nation's air traffic control system have become a leading national security concern. The federal government released a report in 2009 stating that the nation's air traffic control system is vulnerable to a cyber attack that could interrupt communication with pilots and alter the flight information used to separate aircraft as they approach an airport. The report found numerous security problems in airline computer systems, including easy-to-crack passwords and unencrypted file folders, issues that could give invaders easy access. A cyber attack on air traffic has the potential to kill many people and could cripple the country's entire airline industry. Tightening airline computer security could be even more important than conducting security screenings of passengers, because in an increasingly cyber-oriented world, plane hijackers of the future may not even be on board.

a crime. Unless a cryptologist can clearly explain how the science works and how it proves a defendant's innocence or guilt, the evidence will not convince a jury. This has always been a concern for cryptologists who face the task of explaining their methods in court. Even without the added complexity of quantum physics, cryptology can be confounding for judges and juries alike.

Cryptology in the Courtroom

The process of cracking encrypted criminal messages is often long, tedious, and mentally exhausting, even for cryptologists who do it for a living. Explaining cryptology methods to people who have no background in the science can be especially difficult, yet this is necessary when evidence in a criminal court case has resulted from cryptanalysis, whether forensic cryptologists have cracked a criminal's communication or whether they have determined that a criminal has cracked a computer's encryption. Forensic cryptologists often serve as expert witnesses, professionals whose education and experience in a technical area (such as cryptology) qualifies them as specialists whose findings and opinions can be trusted in court. "Judges and juries are not mathematical experts, so they have to rely on statements of experts in cryptology," says computer technology professor Bert-Jaap Koops. But because cryptology evidence results from highly technical procedures that are difficult to explain, he says, the lawyer defending the accused criminal can also cast doubt on the reliability of the evidence. "Perhaps the biggest challenge will be to find expert witnesses who can clearly explain to the judge how encryption and cryptanalysis work."[93]

In a court case where the prosecuting attorney presents evidence against a criminal in the form of messages that have been cryptanalyzed, for example, the prosecution "will have to prove that the resulting cleartext [the cryptanalyzed message] is indeed the original plaintext," says Koops. "The defending attorney may try to discredit this, saying there is no mathematical certainty that the given text is the right plaintext."[94] It is then the expert cryptologist's responsibility to explain exactly how the message was decrypted and why he or she is certain that the decrypted message is actually what the criminal originally wrote. "As it is virtually impossible that a given ciphertext decrypts to two meaningful plaintexts," Koops says, "an expert witness will likely convince the judge of the reliability of the cryptanalysis or decryption."[95] After all, cryptanalysis is not magic, say computer forensic investigators Linda Volnino and Reynaldo Anzaldua. "You can't make things appear that never existed."[96]

Even when the methods used to decrypt criminal communications are shown to be legitimate, however, the methods investigators used to access these communications in the first place may also be questioned in court. The privacy of American citizens is protected by the Fourth Amendment to the U.S. Constitution, which states that people have the right to confidentiality and security in their own homes, documents, and belongings. It protects citizens against unreasonable searches and seizures of their private belongings. In short, if police

Criminal investigators must be careful about how they gather digital evidence or else the evidence may not hold up in a court of law. Software programs such as the one shown are able to gather digital evidence in a way that is legally acceptable to a court.

$20 BILLION

Amount of money the U.S. government will spend by 2025 to upgrade the computer security of the air traffic control system

spy on a suspected criminal's communications without a judge's permission to do so, those communications—however incriminating—cannot be used as evidence against the person if the case goes to court. The efforts of a forensic cryptanalyst will then be wasted, and the criminal may go free. "You don't get a do-over after you compromise [evidence],"[97] say Volnino and Anzaldua. "Legal requirements *always* come first,"[98] they say, because if these laws are ignored or breached, the whole investigation may be thrown out of court.

The Fourth Amendment is perhaps more important for people in the information age than ever before in history. It protects citizens from fearing that their computer communications and data are being spied on by the police and the government. The Fourth Amendment also helps protect people from being accused of information-related crimes they did not commit. Only when criminal investigators can prove to a judge that they have good reasons to suspect someone of criminal activity do they receive a search warrant to intercept and spy on the person's data and communication. The Fourth Amendment "governs much of what police officers are legally allowed to do as they 'serve and protect,'" say criminal justice experts J. Scott Harr and Kären M. Hess. "The idea that citizens can enjoy privacy and freedom from government intrusion with regards to themselves, their possessions, their homes and their businesses is what citizens have come to expect…. If society cannot feel secure from unwarranted invasion by their own government, do any other rights or freedoms really matter?"[99]

Despite the importance of the Fourth Amendment, however, some investigators see it, along with the ever-increasing security of encrypted communication, as a potential shelter for dangerous criminals. They fear that criminals who know they are protected from investigation by the Fourth Amendment and feel comfortable that their communication methods are highly secure because of encryption may use cryptology to plan and carry out crimes on a national scale. Such offenses could affect the security of the entire country. "Although encryption technology holds the promise of giving Internet users freedom from the prying eyes of the government, it also gives terrorists, drug dealers, and [other] criminals a free hand to cause death and destruction without fear of apprehension,"[100] says communications professor Narain Dass Batra. Since the 9/11 terrorist attacks against America, the U.S. government has been increasingly wary of this possibility. The country now faces an ethical dilemma between protecting citizens' privacy and protecting the life and well-being of citizens themselves. "Law-enforcement authorities demand that they be allowed to obtain lawful access to the plain text of encrypted communications data," Batra says, because "without access and other safeguards, the lives of American people will be in danger."[101]

Under the Fourth Amendment, shown here, investigators must prove to a judge that they have good reason to suspect a person of criminal activity in order to gain legal access to the person's data and communications.

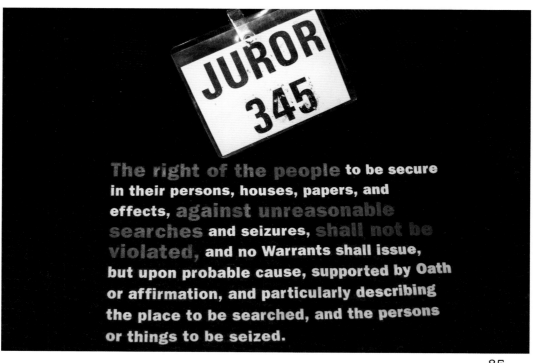

The right of the people to be secure in their persons, houses, papers, and effects, against unreasonable searches and seizures, shall not be violated, and no Warrants shall issue, but upon probable cause, supported by Oath or affirmation, and particularly describing the place to be searched, and the persons or things to be seized.

Cryptology as Patriotism

In 2001, less than two months after the 9/11 terrorist attacks that leveled the World Trade Center and portions of the Pentagon, President George W. Bush signed the USA PATRIOT Act into law. Short for "Uniting and Strengthening America by Providing Appropriate Tools Required to Intercept and Obstruct Terrorism," the Patriot Act gave the government power to discover and take action against terrorists, which the act defines as anyone who commits or is planning to commit dangerous or illegal acts to intimidate the American government or civilians. The legislation also includes laws against cyberterrorism, or hacking into a computer system to carry out terrorist acts (this is now considered a federal crime that can result in a prison sentence of up to twenty years). It even makes the use of encryption methods to cover up criminal plans and communications an illegal activity.

The USA PATRIOT Act makes the use of encryption methods to cover up criminal communications an illegal activity.

The Patriot Act is intended to help the government's law enforcement agencies access certain communications to capture and prosecute criminals, but some say it merely gives government agencies such as the FBI a way around the Fourth Amendment, because they now can eavesdrop on private phone and e-mail communications as long as they claim to suspect that the communicators might be planning terrorist activity. Many Americans think the Patriot Act gives law enforcement far too much access to private information. "The Patriot Act... shifts the FBI's primary function from solving crimes to gathering intelligence within the country," say political scientists Susan Welch, John Gruhl, John Comer, and Susan Rigdon. "The Patriot Act puts in place a surveillance state more extensive than Americans have ever experienced."[102] The act has been harshly criticized for putting law enforcement's needs and desires ahead of the privacy of American citizens.

Another viewpoint, however, is that before the Patriot Act, laws guiding the government's ability to eavesdrop on private communications had not changed much since phone wiretapping laws written in the 1960s. These laws were grossly outdated in a world that has become far more technologically advanced since then. "We are in a peculiar state," says Susan Landau, a computer engineer with Sun Microsystems. "We communicate using mobile phones and laptops, but the laws governing electronic surveillance were developed at a time of fixed-location, circuit-based [phone] systems.... The result is a surveillance regime that may well be out of sync with the times."[103] The FBI believes that a more aggressive stance against criminal communication is essential to prevent terrorism and other serious offenses. "Before the Patriot Act, many of our investigative tools did not account for new communications technologies like e-mail, voicemail, and cell phones, leaving loopholes that terrorists could exploit," says the FBI's Web site, adding that "the Patriot Act made some common sense changes to adapt existing authorities to new technologies." The FBI claims that without the Patriot Act, "our national counterterrorism strategy, which integrates the use of intelligence and law

Terror in Tokyo

On March 20, 1995, a Japanese terrorist group called Aum Shinrikyo released Sarin gas on a subway in Tokyo during the morning commute to work. Originally developed for use as a pesticide, Sarin is a potent and extremely toxic chemical that affects the central nervous system, causing convulsions and tightening of the chest so that a victim can no longer breathe. Twelve people died during the attack, and a thousand others were hospitalized. It was not Aum Shinrikyo's first use of chemical or biological weapons, and it was not meant to be its last. When Japanese authorities confiscated Aum Shinrikyo computers during the investigation, they found files that were masked by complex encryption. Fortunately, they also discovered a floppy disk that had the key for decrypting the files, which contained details of plans to unleash weapons of mass destruction in Japan and the United States. Aum Shinrikyo's use of complex encryption as early as 1995 foreshadowed the increasing role that cryptology would play in masking terrorists' plans in the years ahead.

enforcement tools to prevent attacks, would be unworkable."[104] The need for increased surveillance of terrorist communication is hard to dispute, because encrypted information has, in fact, played a role in plotting serious terrorist attacks in the United States in the past two decades.

Code for Terror

Shortly after noon on February 26, 1993, a bomb exploded in a parking garage beneath one of the Twin Towers of the World Trade Center building in New York City, killing six people and wounding a thousand others. Investigators quickly determined that the bomb was an act of terrorists from the Middle East, some of whom were tracked down after the vehicle identification number of a rented van used in the attack was traced to them. The mastermind of the plot, Ramzi Yousef, had already escaped the country by then, but he was eventually captured in Pakistan in February 1995. His laptop computer was confiscated, and it contained various data files that Yousef had encrypted. When investigators decrypted these files, they discovered that Yousef and his accomplices had been planning other attacks, including the bombing of eleven U.S. airliners. The laptop also contained an encrypted letter describing a plan for terrorists to board five commercial airplanes and detonate bombs on them. American flight schedules, too, were included among Yousef's files.

The 1993 Word Trade Center bombing was the most serious terrorist incident in U.S. history at the time, and the fact that the perpetrators were using encrypted files to mask it and other destructive plans did not escape the attention of law enforcement agencies. "It is imperative that we recognize the needs of law enforcement soon or it will become far more difficult for the FBI…and other federal, state and local law enforcement agencies, faced with the rising threat from the criminal community of commercially available encryption, to protect the public,"[105] said Janet Reno, U.S. Attorney General at the time of the 1993 World Trade Center bombing. When the World Trade Center was again the target of terrorists in 2001, they demolished both Twin Towers, horrifying the world and prompting the U.S. government to create the Patriot Act to combat the rising threat of criminal encryption that Reno had warned about.

Tales of terrorists communicating globally and using highly advanced encryption methods to do so are not hearsay. In 2008 new encryption software was released by an Islamic Web site believed to have connections with al Qaeda, the terrorist group responsible for the 9/11 attacks and many other incidents throughout the world. The new software makes it possible for users to disguise their information with 256-bit encryption. The program can be loaded onto a USB memory stick so that potential terrorists can encrypt e-mails, chat sessions, Web forum postings, and other forms of computer communication from any location and using any computer. The fact that terrorists and other criminals have access to highly advanced encryption methods means that law enforcement agencies cannot rely entirely on intercepting and cracking these criminals' communications to stop them. Instead, they must also bring cryptology full circle and return to cryptography, perfecting even newer and better encryption methods. These will help citizens and organizations protect secret information that terrorists and other criminals could access and use to commit crime and create fear.

An Endless Cycle

Thousands of years have passed since human beings first devised cryptology methods to keep their secret messages hidden from spying eyes, and the state of cryptology has grown from the Caesar cipher, which today's cryptanalysts can crack in mere minutes, to computerized encryption that would take eons to crack by any methods currently available to experts. Cryptology has had important roles in warfare, in crime, and in law enforcement throughout human history, and its impact on public safety has increased vastly during the information age. For each new method that cryptographers devise to mask their messages, cryptanalysts find ways to unmask these messages and get to their secretive contents. The future directions of cryptology are uncertain—they may even delve into physics and leave their mathematical and linguistic roots far behind— but where there are code makers, there will always be code breakers. It is one of the most predictable, if secretive, relationships in forensic science.

Notes

Chapter 1: What is Cryptology?

1. Steven Roger Fischer, *A History of Writing*. London: Reaktion Books, 2003, p. 36.

2. David Kahn, *The Codebreakers: The Comprehensive History of Secret Communication from Ancient Times to the Internet*. New York: Scribner, 1996, p. 72.

3. Kahn, *Codebreakers*, p. 82.

4. Kahn, *Codebreakers*, pp. 83–84.

5. Freidrich Ludwig Bauer, *Decrypted Secrets: Methods and Maxims of Cryptology*, 3rd ed. New York: Springer-Verlag, 2002, p. 7.

6. Tom Wheeler, "How the Telegraph Helped Lincoln Win the Civil War," *George Mason University's History News Network*, November 20, 2006. http://hnn.us/articles/30860.html.

7. Wheeler, "How the Telegraph Helped Lincoln."

8. David Homer Bates, *Lincoln in the Telegraph Office: Recollections of the United States Military Telegraph Corps During the Civil War*. New York: The Century Company, 1907, p. 60.

9. Bates, *Lincoln in the Telegraph Office*, p. 71.

10. Kahn, *Codebreakers*, p. 217.

11. Bauer, *Decrypted Secrets*, p. 6.

12. Bauer, *Decrypted Secrets*, p. 6.

13. Bauer, *Decrypted Secrets*, p. 4.

14. Kahn, *Codebreakers*, p. 124.

15. Cited in an extract from "The Fortieth Congress of the United States," in Thomas Mealey Harris, *Assassination of Lincoln, a History of the Great Conspiracy: Trial of the Conspirators by a Military Commission*. Philadelphia, PA: Historical Publishing Company, 1892, p. 369.

16. John Chandler Griffin, *Abraham Lincoln's Execution*. Gretna, LA: Pelican, 2006, p. 92.

17. Kahn, *Codebreakers*, p. 91.

Chapter 2: How Criminals Use Cryptology

18. James E. Klein, *Grappling with Demon Rum: The Cultural Struggle over Liquor in Early Oklahoma*. Norman, OK: University of Oklahoma Press, 2008, p. 74.

19. Kahn, *Codebreakers*, p. 803.

20. Kahn, *Codebreakers*, p. 804.

21. Quoted in Kahn, *Codebreakers*, p. 804.

22. Kahn, *Codebreakers*, p. 813.

23. Quoted in "Ask the FBI: Codes, Ciphers and Cryptology," *USAToday.com*, January 17, 2002. http://cgi1.usatoday.com/mchat/20020117006/tscript.htm.

24. Controlled Substances Act, 843b, Title 21: Food and Drugs, Chapter 13: "Drug Abuse Prevention and Control," *U.S. Drug Enforcement Agency*. http://www.justice.gov/dea/pubs/csa.html.

25. National Drug Intelligence Center, "Central Valley California High Intensity Drug Trafficking Area Drug Market Analysis 2009," *U.S. Department of Justice*, April 2009. http://www.justice.gov/ndic/pubs32/32767/distribution.htm.

26. Daniel Olson, "Analysis of Criminal Codes and Ciphers," *Forensic Science Communications*, January 2000. http://www.fbi.gov/hq/lab/fsc/backissu/jan2000/olson.htm#code%20systems.

27. Olson, "Criminal Codes and Ciphers."

28. Olson, "Criminal Codes and Ciphers."

29. Olson, "Criminal Codes and Ciphers."

30. Susan A. Phillips, "Graffiti Definition," in *Grove Dictionary of Art*. London: MacMillan, 1996. http://www.graffiti.org/faq/graf.def.html.

31. Robert Walker, "Graffiti," *Gangs Or Us*, http://www.gangsorus.com/graffiti.html.

32. Quoted in Brian Innes, *Serial Killers: The Stories of History's Most Evil Murderers*. London: Quercus, 2007, p. 84.

33. Quoted in Innes, *Serial Killers*, p. 84.

34. Innes, *Serial Killers*, p. 86.

35. Quoted in Innes, *Serial Killers*, p. 86.

36. Innes, *Serial Killers*, p. 86.

37. Robert Graysmith, *Zodiac Unmasked: The Identity of America's Most Elusive Serial Killer Revealed*. New York: Berkley, 2007, p. 189.

38. Quoted in Innes, *Serial Killers*, p. 89.

39. Katharine Ramsland, "The Zodiac Killer: Mystery Has Its Own Allure," *truTV Crime Library*, Turner Broadcasting System. http://www.trutv.com/library/crime/serial_killers/notorious/zodiac/38.html.

40. U.S. Federal Bureau of Investigation, "Today's FBI: Law Enforcement Support and Training," U.S. Department of Justice. http://www.fbi.gov/facts_and_figures/law_enforcement_support.htm

Chapter 3: Cracking Criminal Codes

41. Dorothy E. Denning and William E. Baugh, Jr., "Hiding Crimes in Cyberspace," in *Cybercrime*, edited by Douglas Thomas and Brian D. Loder. New York: Routledge, 2000, p. 110.

42. Denning and Baugh, "Hiding Crimes," p. 110.

43. Denning and Baugh, "Hiding Crimes," p. 106.

44. Denning and Baugh, "Hiding Crimes," p. 109.

45. Denning and Baugh, "Hiding Crimes," p. 111.

46. Quoted in "Ask the FBI."

47. Quoted in "Ask the FBI."

48. Kahn, *Codebreakers*, p. 21.

49. Quoted in "Ask the FBI."

50. Laurence Dwight Smith, *Cryptography: The Science of Secret Writing*. Mineola, NY: Dover, 1955, p. 91.

51. Bauer, *Decrypted Secrets*, pp. 25–26.

52. Reinhard Wobst, *Cryptology Unlocked*, translated by Angelika Shafir. Chichester, UK: John Wiley & Sons, 2007, p. 31.

53. Fred B. Wrixon, *Codes, Ciphers, Secrets, and Cryptic Communication: Making and Breaking Secret Messages from Hieroglyphs to the Internet*. New York: Black Dog & Leventhal, 2005, p. 299.

54. Kahn, *Codebreakers*, p. 99.

55. Kahn, *Codebreakers*, p. 105.

56. Wrixon, *Codes, Ciphers*, p. 299.

57. Wrixon, *Codes, Ciphers*, p. 299.

58. Wrixon, *Codes, Ciphers*, p. 300.

59. Wrixon, *Codes, Ciphers*, p. 300.

60. Kahn, *Codebreakers*, p. 100.

61. Wrixon, *Codes, Ciphers*, p. 302.

62. Wrixon, *Codes, Ciphers*, p. 304.

63. Kahn, *Codebreakers*, p. 105.

64. Kahn, *Codebreakers*, p. 103.

65. Wrixon, *Codes, Ciphers*, p. 303.

66. Quoted in "Ask the FBI."

Chapter 4: Hiding Data from Criminals

67. Jack M. Balkin and Nimrod Kozlovski, "Introduction," in *Cybercrime: Digital Cops and Laws in a Networked Environment*, edited by Jack M. Balkin, James Grimmelman, Eddan Katz, Nimrod Kozlovski, Shlomit Wagman, and Tal Zarsky. New York: New York University Press, 2007, p. 2.

68. Quoted in *Online! The Book*, by John C. Dvorak and Chris Pirillo, Upper Saddle River, NJ: Pearson Education, 2004, p. 308. "Forty Years of Surfing the Internet," *Daily News Los Angeles*, October 29, 2009. http://www.daily-news.com/news/ci_13669715/.

69. Wobst, *Cryptology Unlocked*, p. 1.

70. Quoted in Jason Meserve, "DES Code Cracked in Record Time," *Network World*, January 20, 1999. http://www.networkworld.com/news/1999/0120cracked.html.

71. National Institute of Standards of Technology, "Commerce Secretary Announces New Standard for Global Information Security." http://www.nist.gov/public_affairs/releases/g01-111.cfm.

72. Jeff Tyson, "How Encryption Works," *HowStuffWorks.com*. http://computer

.howstuffworks.com/encryption5 .htm.

73. Debra Littlejohn Shinder, *Scene of the Cybercrime: Computer Forensics Handbook.* Burlington, MA: Syngress Publishing, 2002, p. 305.

74. Shinder, *Scene of the Cybercrime,* p. 306.

75. Shinder, *Scene of the Cybercrime,* p. 307.

76. Shinder, *Scene of the Cybercrime,* p. 307.

77. Michael Cross, *Scene of the Cybercrime,* 2nd edition. Burlington, MA: Syngress Publishing, 2008, p. 484.

78. Cross, *Scene of the Cybercrime,* p. 484.

79. Cross, *Scene of the Cybercrime,* p. 484.

80. Cross, *Scene of the Cybercrime,* p. 484.

81. Wobst, *Cryptology Unlocked,* p. 3.

82. Beryl A. Howell, "Real-World Problems of Virtual Crime," in *Cybercrime: Digital Cops and Laws in a Networked Environment,* edited by Jack M. Balkin, James Grimmelman, Eddan Katz, Nimrod Kozlovski, Shlomit Wagman, and Tal Zarsky. New York: New York University Press, 2007, p. 88.

83. Howell, "Real-World Problems," p. 98.

84. Anthony Reyes and Jack Wiles, *Best Damn Cybercrime and Digital Forensics Book Period.* Burlington, MA: Syngress Publishing, 2007, p. 313.

85. Reyes and Wiles, *Cybercrime and Digital Forensics Book,* pp. 4–5.

86. Andrew Kantor, "It's a Big Internet, But You Can Still Be Tracked Down," *USAToday .com,* June 17, 2004. http://www.usatoday .com/tech/columnist/andrewkantor/ 2004-06-17-kantor_x.htm.

87. Kantor, "Big Internet."

88. Kantor, "Big Internet."

89. Kantor, "Big Internet."

90. Reyes and Wiles, *Cybercrime and Digital Forensics Book,* p. 15.

Chapter 5: The Future of Cryptology

91. Josh Clark, "How Quantum Cryptology Works," *HowStuffWorks.com.* http:// science.howstuffworks.com/quantum-cryptology.htm.

92. Clark, "How Quantum Cryptology Works."

93. Bert-Jaap Koops, *The Crypto-Controversy: A Key Conflict in the Information Society.* The Hague, The Netherlands: Kluwer Law International, 1998, p. 93.

94. Koops, *Crypto-Controversy,* p. 93.

95. Koops, *Crypto-Controversy,* p. 93.

96. Linda Volnino and Reynaldo Anzaldua, *Computer Forensics for Dummies.* Hoboken NJ: Wiley Publishing, 2008, p. 15.

97. Volnino and Anzaldua, *Computer Forensics for Dummies,* p. 14.

98. Volnino and Anzaldua, *Computer Forensics for Dummies,* p. 40.

99. J. Scott Harr and Kären M. Hess, *Constitutional Law and the Criminal Justice System*, 4th edition. Belmont, CA: Thomson Higher Education, 2008, p. 176.

100. N. D. Batra, *Digital Freedom: How Much Can You Handle?*. Lanham, MD: Rowman & Littlefield, 2008, p. 108.

101. Batra, *Digital Freedom*, p. 108.

102. Susan Welch, John Gruhl, John Comer, and Susan Rigdon, *Understanding American Government*, 12th edition. Boston, MA: Wadsworth, 2010, p. 443.

103. Susan Landau, "Security, Liberty, and Electronic Communications," in *Advances in Cryptology: CRYPTO 2004*, proceedings of the 24th Annual International Cryptology Conference in Santa Barbara, CA, August 2004, edited by Matthew Franklin. Berlin, Germany: Springer, 2004, pp. 355–56.

104. Federal Bureau of Investigation, "USA Patriot Act," U.S. Department of Justice. http://www.fbi.gov/aboutus/transformation/patriot_act.htm.

105. Testimony before the House Select Committee on Intelligence in June 1999, quoted in Jake Tapper, "Don't Blame It on Reno," *Salon*, January 2, 2002. http://www.salon.com/news/politics/feature/2002/01/02/reno.

Glossary

Advanced Encryption Standard (AES): The government's current recommended method for encrypting computerized data securely.

algorithm: Mathematical method for encrypting and decrypting data in a computer; a key.

alphanumeric: Containing both letters and numbers.

anagramming: Replacing the letters of a cryptogram or cipher to reveal the true message.

bit: Short for *binary digit*; the smallest unit of information used by a computer.

brute force method: Solving an encrypted message by trying every possible solution.

cipher: A disguised text in which individual letters have been replaced with other letters, numbers, or symbols.

code: A system of disguising language by replacing entire words or phrases with other words, phrases, or symbols.

conspirator: Someone who works secretly with others to commit a crime or carry out an illegal act.

cryptanalysis: Solving ciphers or other forms of secret writing without knowing the method used to create them.

cryptogram: A text disguised by a cipher or code.

cryptography: The writing of messages in cipher or code, or the computerized enciphering of data.

cryptology: The scientific study of cryptography and cryptanalysis, or creating and solving codes and ciphers.

cybercrime: Crime committed using a computer, and usually, the Internet.

cyberterror: The use of computers or the Internet as tools to carry out acts of terrorism.

Data Encryption Standard (DES): The encryption method the U.S. government recommended for protecting computerized data from 1977 to 2000.

decryption: Solving a cipher or other form of secret writing when one knows the correct method, or key, used to create it.

digital signature: An electronic tag, unique to a single computer user, that can be added to a data file and cannot be forged or deleted.

encryption: Writing a message in code or cipher; cryptography.

expert witness: A person who specializes in a certain subject and testifies in a

96

trial to explain the subject to the judge and jury.

extortion: The use of force, intimidation, or power to make someone else do something or give up something.

forensic cryptology: The study and analysis of codes and ciphers used in criminal acts.

fraud: A type of deceit in which a person pretends to be someone else for money or personal gain.

frequency chart: A chart created by cryptanalysts that shows the frequency of each symbol used in a given cipher.

Internet protocol address: A unique number assigned to a computer that allows it to access and receive data from the Internet.

key: The method by which a code or cipher can be solved.

linguistics: The study of the structure of human language.

local area network (LAN): A group of computers that share a common communication link.

message digest: An encrypted summary of a data file that, once attached to the file, cannot be changed even if the original message is changed.

password cracking: The process of recovering a computer password through cryptanalysis.

photon: The smallest known unit of light.

plaintext: The undisguised text of a message before it is encrypted and after it has been decrypted.

probability: The chance that a particular event will occur.

public-key encryption: A method of cryptography that encrypts data with two different keys so it can be passed safely from one user to another over the Internet.

statistics: The collection and analysis of numerical data.

steganography: Concealing the existence of a message within an object, a text, or an image.

terrorism: The use of violence or threats of violence against a government or civilians to achieve a personal or political goal.

For More Information

Books

Richard Belfield, *The Six Unsolved Ciphers: Inside the Mysterious Codes That Have Confounded the World's Greatest Cryptographers*. Berkeley, CA: Ulysses Press, 2007, 312 pp. This book tells the stories of a handful of the most notorious ciphers in history, including those of the Zodiac Killer and the unsolved Beale ciphers that are said to contain the secret location of a treasure buried somewhere in Virginia.

The Diagram Group and David Lambert, *Super Little Giant Book of Secret Codes*. New York: Sterling Publishing, 2007, 288 pp. Step-by-step instructions are given for trying out dozens of systems of secret writing as well as a brief history of each system.

Ben Hubbard, *High Tech World: Codebreakers*. New York: Crabtree Publishing, 2010, 32 pp. This book offers young readers a brief history of code breaking, from the Enigma code breakers of World War II to modern-day cybercrime.

Paul B. Janeczko, *Top Secret: A Handbook of Codes, Ciphers and Secret Writing*. Cambridge, MA: Candlewick Press, 2006, 144 pp. This book describes different types of codes and ciphers and their history and includes activities such as making invisible ink and various other devices to conceal writing.

Articles

"The Future of Privacy: Can We Safeguard Our Information in a High-Tech, Insecure World?," *Scientific American*, Special Issue, September 2008. Every article in this issue of *Scientific American* discusses some aspect of information security. Topics include cryptography, digital surveillance, social networking sites, and Internet eavesdropping.

Web Sites

Central Intelligence Agency (CIA) Kids Page (https://www.cia.gov/kids-page/index.html). The CIA kids' page takes visitors inside the CIA, describing the history of the organization and what its agents do. There is a section of puzzles and games that includes several cipher-breaking challenges.

CryptoKids (http://www.nsa.gov/kids/). This kids' page of the National Security Agency Web site explains codes and ciphers and gives examples of how they are made and broken. It includes games and challenges as well as a section about the National Security Agency and its role in protecting America.

National Cryptologic Museum (http://www.nsa.gov/about/cryptologic_heritage/museum/index.shtml). The National Cryptologic Museum is in Fort Meade, Maryland, but visitors to the Web site can take a virtual tour of its most popular exhibits chronicling the history of cryptology in America. The virtual tour features sections on women and African Americans in cryptology, American wars, computers in cryptology, and much more.

DVDs

Modern Marvels: Codes. New York: History Channel, 2006, 50 minutes. Cryptologists explain the history and development of cryptology, using examples such as Caesar's ancient ciphers and the codes of World War II, and end with a discussion of cyberspace and computerized encryption.

Index

Advanced Encryption Standard (AES), 65–66, 77, 80

Aeneas the Tactician, 13

AES (Advanced Encryption Standard), 65–66, 77, 80

Air traffic computer security, 81

American Civil War, 17–19, *18*, 25–27

Ames, Aldrich, 45

Anzaldua, Reynaldo, 83, 84

ARPAnet, 62

Aum Shinrikyo, 88

Bach, Johann Sebastian, 32

Baker, Lafayette, *26*, 27

Balkin, Jack M., 61

Bates, Cheri Jo, 38–39

Batra, Narain Dass, 85

Bauer, Friedrich Ludwig, 16, 21, 23, 53

Baugh, William E. Jr., 45–46

Binary code, *64*

Brucia, Carlie, 43–44

Caesar cipher, *14*, 15–16

CCRU (Cryptanalysis and Racketeering Unit), 43–44

Central Intelligence Agency (CIA), 45

Certified Forensic Computer Examiner (CFCE), 72

Chemical weapons, 88

CIA (Central Intelligence Agency), 45

Cipher, 14–15, *42*, *52*, *54*
See also computer-made codes and ciphers; cryptography

Civil War, 17–19, *18*, 25–27

Clark, Josh, 77–78

Coast Guard, 30–32

Code. *See* cipher

CodeTalkers, *22*

Comer, John, 87

Computer-made codes and ciphers, 63–66

Controlled Substances Act, 33–34

Covert secret writing, 32

Credit card fraud, 71–73

Cross, Michael, 69

Cryptanalysis
  career information, 47
  clues, 56–60
  computer technology, 60
  criminal confessions, 43–44
  definition, 9
  nature of work, 49, 52–59

requirements for career, 47–49

work environment, 48–49, *50*, 50–51

Cryptanalysis and Racketeering Unit (CCRU), 43–44

Cryptogram, *15*, *42*

Cryptography
  ancient civilizations, 12
  criminal investigations, 42
  definition, 9
  quantum computers, 77–82, *79*

Cryptology
  alcohol smuggling, 28–33
  ancient civilizations, 11–16
  crime association, 23, 27
  criminology, 23
  cybercrime relationship, 61–66
  cybercrime solutions, 73–76
  definition, 11
  drug trade, 33–36
  elections, 51
  espionage association, 23
  evidence, *42*
  expert witnesses, 82–83
  forensic, 23, 46
  graffiti, 36–38
  homicide, 38–44

legal system relationship, 82–85

murder, 38–44

overview, 8–10, 90

patriotism relationship, 86–88

purposes, 12

quantum, 77–82

serial killings, 38–44

smuggling, 28–36

text messages, 35

treason, 23–25

warfare role in development, 19–23

World War II, *50*, 50–51

Cybercrime, 61–66, 70–76
See also hacking

Cybercrime investigator, 72

Data Encryption Standard (DES), 64–65

Data protection, *66*, *68*, 68–69, 70–73

Davis, Jefferson, 26–27

Decryption, 16–17, *56*, 56–59

On the *Defense of Fortified Places* (Aeneas the Tactician), 13

Denning, Dorothy, 45–46

DES (Data Encryption Standard), 64–65

Digital evidence, 82–85, *83*, *85*

Digital security, 61–76

Digital signature, 75–76

DNA evidence, 43–44

Drug trade, *33*, 33–35

Egyptians, 11, 12

Eighteenth Amendment (of U.S. Constitution), 28–33

Elizabeth I, 23, 25

Email encryption, 78

Enciphering. *See* encryption

Encoding. *See* encryption

Encryption, 16, 17, *52*, 52–55
emails, 78

Enigma cipher machine, *20*, 21

Espionage, 45

ETAONRISH, 57
See also decryption

Expert witnesses, 82–83

Extortion, 70–71

FBI (Federal Bureau of Investigation), 33, 43–44, 45, 46, 87–88

Fischer, Steven Roger, 11

Forensic cryptology, 23, 46
See also legal system

Fourth Amendment (of U.S. Constitution), 83–85

Fraud, 71–73

Frequency charts, 57

Friedman, Elizabeth, 31–32

Future. *See* quantum cryptography

Gangs, 36–38

"The Gold Bug" (Poe), 55

Gonzalez, Albert, 72
See also hacking

Graffiti, 36–38, *37*

Graysmith, Robert, 40–41, *41*

Great Depression, 36

Greeks, 12–13, 17

Griffin, John Chandler, 27

Gruhl, John, 87

Hacking, 62, 67–68, *69*, 72–73

Harden, Donald, 39, 40, 47

Harr, J. Scott, 84

Hess, Kären M., 84

Homicide, 38–44

Howell, Beryl A., 70–71

Information age, 61

Information Society Project, 61

International Association of Computer Investigative Specialists, 72

Internet, 61–63

Internet Crime Complaint Center, 69

IP (Internet Protocol) address, *74*, 74–75

Johnson, Andrew, 27

Julius Caesar, 15–16

Justice system, 82–85

Kaczynski, Theodore, 42

Kahn, David
on criminals and cryptology, 30–31, 32
on cryptograms, 54–55, 58

on history of cryptology, 12, 13, 15–16, 19, 25, 27
Kantor, Andrew, 74–75
Klein, James, 29
Kozlovski, Nimrod, 61

LAN (local-area network), 67
Landau, Susan, 87
Legal system, 82–85
Lincoln, Abraham, 25–27
Local-area network (LAN), 67

Mary, Queen of Scots, 23, 24, 25, 49
McNett, David, 65
Medieval ciphers, 23–25
Mesopotamians, 11
Message digest, 76

National Drug Intelligence Center, 34
National Institute of Standards and Technology (NIST), 65–66
National Prohibition Act, 29
National Security Agency (NSA), 46
Navajo CodeTalkers, 22, 22
9/11 events. *See* September 11, 2001 events
1993 World Trade Center bombing, 89
See also September 11, 2001 events

NIST (National Institute of Standards and Technology), 65–66
NSA (National Security Agency), 46

"Password cracking," 67–68
Password protection, 66
Passwords, 66, 66–70, 68
Patriot Act, 86, 86–88, 89
Patriotism, 86–88
Photons, 79–80
Physics, 79, 81–82
See also quantum computers
Poe Cryptographic Challenge, 55
Poe, Edgar Allen, 55
Police, 49–50, 75, 84
Polybius, 13
Polybius Square, 13
Poulsen, Kevin, 62
Privacy issues, 83–85
Prohibition, 28–33
Purple ciphering process, 21

Quantum computers, 77–79
Quantum cryptography, 77–82, 79
Quantum cryptology, 77–82
Quantum physics, 79, 81–82

Reno, Janet, 89
Reyes, Anthony, 73, 76
Rigdon, Susan, 87

Riverside Press-Enterprise, 38–39
Romans, 13–14, 17
Rumrunning, 28–33, 30

San Francisco Chronicle, 39, 40
San Francisco Examiner, 39
September 11, 2001 events, 81, 88–89
Shinder, Debra Littlejohn, 67–68
"Skytale," 13
Smith, Joe, 43–44
Smith, Laurence Dwight, 49
Smuggling. *See* drug trade; rumrunning
Spartans, 13
Speakeasies, 29
Spying, 45
Stanton, Edward M., 27
Steganography, 32
Street gangs, 36–38

Telegraph, 17–19, 18
Terrorism, 88
See also September 11, 2001 events
Text messages, 35
Tomlinson, Roy, 62
Twenty-first Amendment (of U.S. Constitution), 32–33
Tyler, W.B., 55
Tyson, Jeff, 66

Unabomber, 42

Undercover agents, 49–50
U.S. Coast Guard, 30–32
USA PATRIOT Act, *86*,
  86–88, 89

Vallejo Times-Herald, 39
Volnino, Linda, 83, 84

Walker, Robert, 37–38

Welch, Susan, 87
Wheeler, Tom, 18
Wiles, Jack, 73, 76
Wobst, Reinhard, 63, 70
World Trade Center,
  88–89
  See also September 11, 2001
  events
World War I, 17, 31

World War II, 19–23, *50*,
  50–51
Wrixon, Fred, 54–55, 57–58

Yousef, Ramzi, 89
  See also terrorism

Zodiac cipher, *39*, 39–41, *41*

Picture Credits

About the Author

Jenny MacKay has written nine nonfiction books for teens and is a fan of true crime stories. She and her family live in northern Nevada.